Tipbook Music on Paper
Basic Theory

Woodbourne Library
Washington-Centerville Public Library
Centerville, Ohio

Publishing Details

This first edition published November 2002 by
The Tipbook Company bv, The Netherlands.

Distributed exclusively by the Hal Leonard Corporation,
7777 West Bluemound Road, P.O. Box 13819
Milwaukee, Wisconsin 53213.

Typeset in Glasgow and Minion.

Printed in The Netherlands by Hentenaar Boek bv, Nieuwegein.

144pp

ISBN 90-76192-32-4

Hugo Pinksterboer

Tipbook
Music on
Paper
Basic Theory

**An easy-to-read guide for anyone
who wants to learn how to read music, and a handy
reference book for anyone who already can.**

THE **TIPBOOK** COMPANY

THE BEST GUIDE TO YOUR INSTRUMENT!

Thanks

Many thanks go to trumpeter and teacher Bart Noorman, who supplied a great deal of the information gathered in this book, and to Duncan Clark for his valuable additions.

For their information, their expertise, their time, and their help we'd also like to thank the following musicians, teachers, and other experts: Steve Clover, Elliot Freedman, Gerard Braun, Davina Cowan, Theo Olof, John van der Veer, Jeroen Brinkhof, Edwin Dijkman, Dirk Hooglandt, Tamara Santing, Hinke Wever, Dick Barten, Heske Berkenkamp, Harm van der Geest, Dick Kuijs, Willem Lohy, Leon van Mil, Tijn Sardée, Carin Tielen, and Will Vermeer.

Anything missing?

Any omissions? Any areas that could be improved? Please go to www.tipbook.com to contact us; thanks!

The makers

Journalist and musician **Hugo Pinksterboer**, author and editor of *The Tipbook Series* has published hundreds of interviews, articles, and instrument, video, CD, and book reviews for Dutch and international music magazines. He is the author of the reference work for cymbals (*The Cymbal Book*, Hal Leonard).

Illustrator, designer, and musician **Gijs Bierenbroodspot** has worked as an art director for a wide variety of magazines and has developed numerous ad campaigns. While searching in vain for information about saxophone mouthpieces, he got the idea for this series of books on music and musical instruments. He is responsible for the layout and illustrations of all of the Tipbooks.

Acknowledgements

Cover photo: René Vervloet
Editor: Robert L. Doerschuk
Proofreader: Nancy Bishop

IN BRIEF

Tipbook Music on Paper – Basic Theory is a highly accessible introduction to reading music from the very first start, as well as a handy reference guide if you can already read music. It also explains the basic principles of music theory, from scales and keys to transposition and the circle of fifths.

Easier
This book helps you to understand more about what you're playing, which in turn makes it easier to read music, and to play music in almost any style. It is full of easy-to-play examples and practical tips – and it's not just about theory, it's about music.

Any style, any instrument
Tipbook Music on Paper – Basic Theory has been written for musicians in any style, from rock guitarists to classical flutists, and of any age, and it's being used by absolute beginners as well as advanced instrumentalists and singers.

Glossary
The first chapter explains the plan of the book. The glossary and the list of signs and markings at the end of the book provide quick access to many questions; the glossary doubles as an index.

Hugo Pinksterboer

CONTENTS

HEAR WHAT YOU READ WITH TIPCODE

www.tipbook.com

Tipbooks offer you a new way to hear what you are reading about. The Tipcodes that you will come across regularly in this book give you access to soundtracks and other additional information at www.tipbook.com.

How it works is very simple. One example: On page 26 of this book you can read about quintuplets and septuplets. Right above that paragraph it says **Tipcode MOP-016**. Type

First, make your selection: Tipcode, chords, and fingering charts, or the glossary.

The Tipcode window displays movies, photo series, fingering charts, chords, and explanations of the words used in this book.

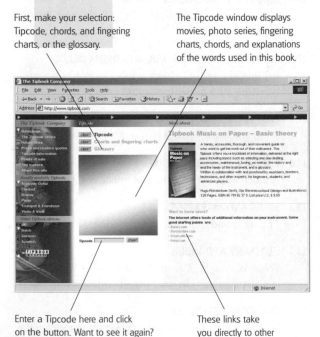

Enter a Tipcode here and click on the button. Want to see it again? Click again.

These links take you directly to other interesting sites.

in that code on the Tipcode page at www.tipbook.com and you will hear what a quintuplet and a septuplet sound like.

Enter code and listen
You enter the Tipcode beneath the movie window on the Tipcode page. In most cases, you will hear the relevant audio example within a few seconds.

Combined
In some cases, a number of audio examples has been combined in a single Tipcode. One Tipcode in this book activates a short movie instead of a soundtrack.

Plug-ins
If the software you need to hear these soundtracks is not yet installed on your computer, you'll automatically be told which programs you need, and where you can download them. This kind of software (*plug-ins*) is free.

Still more at www.tipbook.com
You can find even more information at www.tipbook.com. For instance, you can look up words in the glossaries of all the Tipbooks published to date. And for guitarists and pianists there are chord diagrams; for saxophonists, clarinetists, and flutists there are fingering charts; for drummers there are the rudiments.

1. MUSIC ON PAPER

Learning to read music is not much harder than is was to learn reading English. You started off with one letter at a time, then moved up to reading words, and now you handle entire phrases at a glance. And just like learning to read English, it takes a little time at first, but it definitely pays off in the end. An introduction, and how to get the most out of this book.

Lots of famous musicians have never read a note in their lives. Not among classical musicians, but in other styles, from rock to house to jazz, there are plenty. Thousands of groups and bands don't have a single member who reads music. And there are thousands of songs thought up by musicians who never put anything down on paper. But if you *do* read music…

- You'll have access to **loads of sheet music**, including songs and pieces by your favorite band or composer, as well as study material.
- You'll be able to **play along** with groups who use sheet music right away.
- You can also **write music** – exercises and tunes, a part for the bass player or the brass section, an idea for a solo. Writing something down is easier than remembering it, especially in the long run.
- Talking to other musicians is a **lot easier**. You'll never be dumbstruck by talk of a Bb-major scale, a fifth, a triplet, or the Mixolydian mode.
- It's easier to **understand how music is structured** – from single chords to whole pieces – and how and why it works the way it does.

1

By heart

Being able to read music doesn't mean you always have to play from paper. Classical musicians usually do, but music stands are rare on rock, blues, and folk stages. Sheet music allows you to play things that others have written, but once you know a piece by heart, it may very well sound better if you play it without the music: You'll be able to concentrate on how the notes are supposed to sound, rather than on which ones you're supposed to play.

WHERE WHAT CAN BE FOUND

The first chapters of this book concentrate on learning to read music. Chapters 2 and 3 look at how high or low the

The numbers in the black circles indicate the relevant chapter for each subject.

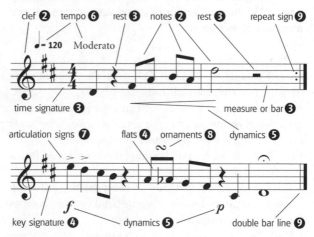

- The clef and the staff: **Chapter 2**
- The higher the position of a note on the staff, the higher it sounds: **Chapter 2**
- The looks of notes and rests tell you how long they last: **Chapter 3**
- The number of beats per bar, and which note lasts one beat: **Chapter 3**
- Notes can be raised or lowered a half tone by using sharps and flats: **Chapter 4**

- Dynamic markings tell you to play loud, or soft, or at any volume level in between: **Chapter 5**
- Tempo indications show how fast a piece should be played: **Chapter 6**
- Accents and other articulation markings show how a note should be 'pronounced': **Chapter 7**
- Ornaments are used to embellish notes: **Chapter 8**
- Repeat signs tell you to repeat one or more bars: **Chapter 9**

notes sound (pitch), how long they last, and when to play them. Chapters 4 to 8 tell you *how* you should play them: loud, soft, fast or slow, accented, or embellished. Chapter 9 covers repeat signs and section markings. The guide on the opposite page summarizes where each bit of information can be found.

Ten to fourteen

Chapters 10 to 14 explain the system behind the notes. You don't necessarily need all this information to read music 'note by note,' but it definitely helps to really understand what you're playing.

Fifteen and onwards

Chapters 15 to 20 are extras, covering transposition, unusual meters, swing, the clave, 'noteless' ways to put music on paper, musical notation for drummers, tips on writing out music, and a brief history of music notation.

Keyboard instrument and Tipcode

Having a keyboard instrument at hand makes this book even more instructive – even if you can play it with one finger only. A very basic home keyboard, available for as little as fifty dollars, is all you need. Note that the Tipcodes in this book allow you to listen to most of the musical examples at www.tipbook.com (see page VIII).

A basic, small keyboard is all you need to play the examples in this book.

Compositions and numbers

A piece of classical music is usually called a *composition*. Pop songs, jazz standards, and other compositions are usually referred to as *songs* or *tunes*. In this book, the neutral term *piece* is used in most cases, for compositions in any style of music. A *chart, part,* or *score* contains the written music for a specific instrument. The word *score* is also often used to indicate the conductor's sheet music, which shows all the parts in a piece.

'Twinkle, Twinkle, Little Star'

This book begins with 'Twinkle, Twinkle, Little Star' and a few other well-known children's songs. Why? Simply because they are familiar to everyone – and it's a lot easier to grasp what you read if you already know what it's supposed to sound like.

Western and non-Western music

Tipbook Music on Paper – Basic Theory deals with what's known as Wsestern music – music that could best be described as originating from Europe and the United States. Non-Western music can be heard increasingly often in Western countries, either in pure form or mixed with Western elements. In many cases, different rules apply to these musical styles, ranging from different notation to completely different ways to compose or structure the music.

2. HIGH AND LOW

Bass guitars produce lower notes than violins. Trumpets sound higher notes than tubas. But all these instruments can play both high and low notes. If you look at a piece of music on paper, the high notes are printed 'higher' than the low notes. This chapter covers how the different notes, from high to low, are indicated on paper.

On a keyboard instrument, every note has its own key. Having one at hand (see page 3) is of great help for the following introduction.

Twinkle, Twinkle
Tipcode MOP-001

If you sing 'Twinkle, Twinkle, Little Star,' the second 'twinkle' sounds higher than the first. If you play it on a keyboard

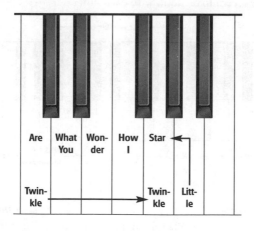

'Twinkle, Twinkle, Little Star': Each syllable is a note.

5

instrument, you'll see that you find the higher sounding notes by moving to the right along the keyboard. Move to the left, and the notes sound lower.

On the keyboard

The diagram on the previous page shows you how to play this song on a keyboard instrument. For every syllable, simply play the key on which it's written.

Higher is faster

If you play a higher sounding note on a piano, the piano's strings vibrate faster. If you sing a higher note, your vocal folds vibrate faster. Stretch a rubber band, make it vibrate as if it were a string, and listen to the sound. Now stretch it a bit further. You'll see that it starts vibrating faster, and you'll hear a higher pitch.

The octave   Tipcode MOP-002

If you sing *do, re, mi, fa, so, la, ti, do* (*i.e.,* an *ascending* scale), at the last *do* your vocal folds will vibrate twice as fast as at the first *do*. In musical terms: The high *do* sounds an *octave* higher than the first.

The same, but higher

The high *do* is the same note as the low *do*, but at a higher pitch. When you play these two notes simultaneously on a piano, you'll hardly hear that you're playing two notes: They seem to blend in with each other,

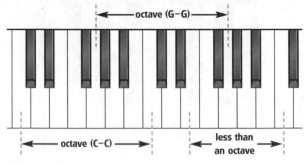

Octaves on a keyboard.

An octave   Tipcode MOP-003

If you want to play an octave on a piano or another keyboard instrument, you simply play any white key, and then play the key you find by counting eight white keys up (including the first one). In other words: An octave encompasses eight white notes.

Letter names

The white keys all have a letter name: C, D, E, F, G, A, and B. These are *natural notes* or *white notes*. From one C to the next C is an octave; from one D to the next D is an octave too; and so on.

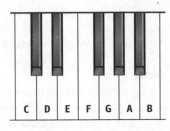

The seven white notes or natural notes.

Black keys   Tipcode MOP-004

A keyboard also has black keys. If you go from key to key, white and black, from left to right, every next note will be a *half tone* or a *half step* higher. On a piano keyboard, a half step is the smallest distance between two notes. There are twelve half steps in an octave.

Whole steps

If you go from one white key to the next, the diagram below shows that you play both half steps and whole steps.

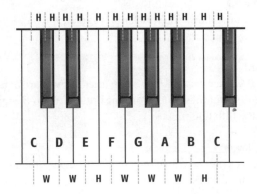

From key to key: half steps (H). From white key to white key: whole (W) and half (H) steps.

Finding your way

The black keys on a keyboard are laid out in alternate groups of two and three. This layout makes all the notes very easy to find. Two examples? The white key just before *two* black keys is always a C. And the white keys just before each group of *three* black keys are the F's on the keyboard.

Middle C

The C in the middle of a piano keyboard is *Middle C*. Middle C is also known as C4: It's the fourth C on the keyboard, counting from left to right.

Guitar

The guitar is another instrument on which half and whole steps can be easily played. If you slide your finger upward from fret to fret (from the top of the neck toward the body), you'll be moving up in half steps. If you move up twelve frets (twelve half steps), you play an octave. If you skip one fret each time, you're moving up in whole steps or whole tones.

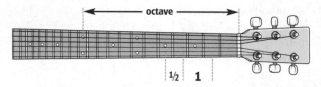

Whole steps, half steps, and an octave on guitar.

ON PAPER

Written music shows you which notes to play, and how long each note should last.

The staff

Music is written on a *staff* or *stave*: a set of five horizontal lines. You count these lines from the bottom up, so the top line is the fifth line.

Higher, lower

The higher a note is written on the staff, the higher it sounds. Lower-sounding notes sit lower on the staff.

Left to right

You read and play the notes from left to right, just like words.

How long

The appearance of each note tells you how long it's supposed to last. For example, there are notes with an open head, with a closed head and a stem, and so on. This is dealt with in Chapter 3.

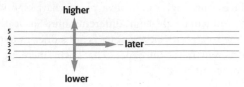

Up, down, and to the right.

On paper

Tipcode MOP-005

The following example shows you what 'Twinkle, Twinkle' looks like in notes. When the melody goes up, the notes on the staff go up too. And as the tune goes down (from 'little'), the corresponding notes are lower on the staff.

Music on paper: a higher note is higher on the staff.

Lines and spaces

A staff can house eleven notes. They can be written either
• on the lines (the line runs through the note);
• in the spaces between the lines; or
• below or above the lines.

Notes on the lines.

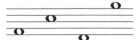

Notes between, below, or above the lines.

Eleven notes on the staff.

9

CLEFS

On a bass guitar you play very low notes, and a violin produces only high ones. Most pianos have eighty-eight keys, producing eight-eight different notes. So clearly, one five-lined staff with eleven notes is not sufficient to put all the different notes on paper. That's why there are staffs with different *clefs*.

G-clef and F-clef

The clef is the symbol at the beginning of a staff. The two most common clefs are the curly *G-clef* and the *F-clef*, which looks somewhat like a big comma.

Treble clef

The staff with the G-clef is used for high-sounding notes: Music for high-sounding instruments, such as trumpets and violins, is written on a staff with this clef. Therefore it's also known as the *treble clef*.

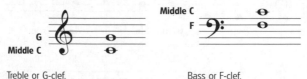

Treble or G-clef.   Bass or F-clef.

Curl

The curl of the G-clef or treble clef indicates the note G above Middle C. Middle C is below this staff.

Bass clef

The staff with the F-clef is used for lower-sounding instruments, such as the bass and the tuba. Therefore it's also known as the *bass clef*.

Two dots

The two dots of the F-clef indicate the note F below Middle C. Middle C is above this staff.

Notes and keys   Tipcode MOP-006

The following diagrams shows some piano keys and the corresponding notes on the staffs. As you can see, Middle C has its own line in between the two staffs. Note that the dots of the F-clef point at the line for a low F; the curl of the G-clef marks the line for a high G.

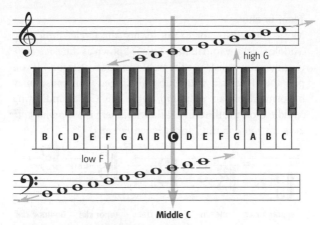

Natural notes in the bass (F) and treble (G) clefs.

Different

So the notes sit on different places on each staff. For example, the middle line of the treble staff indicates a G. The middle line of the bass clef indicates a D.

Both staffs   Tipcode MOP-007

Most musicians only need to learn to read the notes in one of these staffs. If you play the piano or another keyboard instrument you'll have to read both staffs simultaneously: the one with a bass clef for the lower sounding notes you play with your left hand, and the treble clef to indicate the higher-sounding notes you usually play with your right hand. Harpists also have to read both staffs.

Pianists read two staffs simultaneously: Here's a bit of salsa for advanced players.

C-clef

There is yet another clef, the *C-clef*. It indicates Middle C. Contrary to the other clefs, it is a *moveable clef*. It can assign the note C to any of the five lines of the staff.

11

Tenor or alto

Music for cellists, for example, has the C-clef indicating Middle C on the fourth line. This is known as the *tenor staff*. (Incidentally, cellists use the treble and bass clefs too.) If you play the viola or if you're an alto singer, your music may be printed on an *alto staff*, with the C-clef indicating Middle C on the third line. Likewise, there is a *soprano staff*, a *mezzo-soprano staff*, and a *baritone staff*.

soprano clef   mezzo-soprano clef   alto clef   tenor clef   baritone clef

The C-clef or moveable clef: Middle C can be assigned to any line.

Treble clef

Most examples in this book use the treble staff, which is the most commonly used staff.

EXTENDING THE STAFFS

Using different clefs isn't enough to represent the highest and the lowest notes on paper. Therefore, the staffs can be extended in two ways.

Ledger lines

Each staff can be extended with small lines, called *ledger lines*. Middle C is always on a ledger line, below the treble staff and above the bass staff.

Notes on ledger lines.

Octave higher or lower

Some notes require three or more ledger lines. That makes reading them quite hard. The solution is simple: Instead of writing a note far above or below the staff, you're told to play an octave – or even two octaves – higher or lower than what's actually written.

- The symbol 8*va* (*ottava*) or the number 8 above a note indicates that this and the notes that follow should be played an octave higher than written.
- If you're required to play an octave lower, one of the following symbols is written under the first note: 8va bassa, 8*vb* (*ottava bassa*), or the number 8.
- If the 8 is replaced by 15 in any of these markings, you have to play two octaves higher or lower.

Two ways of writing the same melody. The one below is much easier to read.

Loco

From the marking, there's usually a line to tell you how long to continue playing higher or lower (as shown above). If there's no line, you continue until you see the Italian word *loco*.

AND MORE

Two final points on transposing instruments and chords.

Transposing instruments

Most wind instruments sound a different note than the one written down. An example: If you play the tenor saxophone and there is a C in your chart, you will finger a C – but the pitch you will hear sounds a whole step lower. This is because the tenor saxophone, like most other wind instruments, is a *transposing instrument*. There's more about this in Chapter 15. Non-transposing instruments are said to play in *concert pitch*.

Chords   Tipcode MOP-008

On keyboard instruments, guitars, and many other stringed instruments, you can play *chords*: two, but usually three or more notes played simultaneously. On paper, the notes of a chord are aligned vertically. If two notes occupy adjacent places on the staff, they can't be aligned vertically, so they're printed very close to one another instead. There's more about chords in chapter 18.

A chord is a number of notes played simultaneously.

3. LONG AND SHORT

The position of a note on the staff shows you which note to play. The look of the note itself tells you how long it's supposed to last.

Whether you are listening to drum 'n' bass, a symphony orchestra, jazz, or country – you can always tap your foot in time to what you hear. Once every few taps you may hear or feel some sort of accent. Just sing the two following songs:

1 - 2   1 - 2   1 - 2   1

Yan-kee **Doo**-dle **went** to **town**.

1 - 2 - 3 **1** -2 - 3 **1**- 2-(3)

(My) **Bon**-nie lies **o**-ver the **o**-cean.

Oompa

The 'accents' in 'Yankee Doodle' subdivide the song into groups of two taps or beats. 'My Bonnie' is divided into groups of three beats. These subdivisions determine the rhythmic 'feel' of the music. Dance to it and you'll feel it: *oompa oompa* makes you move differently than *oompapa oompapa* does.

Bars

Most music is divided into such groups of two, three, or four beats. Each group of beats is called a *bar* or a *measure*.

THE NOTES

Tipcode MOP-009

If you clap along as you sing the first four words of 'Bah bah black sheep' you will probably clap on each word. 'Bah Bah Black Sheep' is four beats.

Quarter note

The example below shows how these four beats look on paper. Each beat is represented by a black bullet with a stem, known as a *quarter note*. In the majority of songs and classical pieces, the quarter note represents one beat.

Four in a bar

In most of those songs and compositions, there are four quarter notes to every bar. This is shown at the beginning of the staff as $\frac{4}{4}$.

Longer and shorter

The second line of 'Bah Bah Black Sheep' has words that last shorter and longer than one beat. To indicate these longer and shorter durations, there are whole, half, eighth, sixteenth and other notes.

The whole note: four beats in $\frac{4}{4}$

Tipcode MOP-010

The longest note you can play in a bar of four beats is the *whole note*. The *whole* note fills up the *whole* bar. If you play a whole note on a keyboard, you hold the key down for all four beats. On a wind instrument, you keep blowing for four beats. Tapping your foot, one tap per beat, will help you counting out the note.

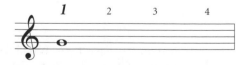

A whole note lasts four beats in $\frac{4}{4}$.

The half note: two beats in ⁴₄

The *half note* lasts half as long as a whole note: two beats. Two half notes fill up a four-beat bar.

The half note: two beats in ⁴₄.

The quarter note: one beat in ⁴₄

In ⁴₄ the *quarter note* lasts one beat. If you tap along with your foot, play one note to each tap.

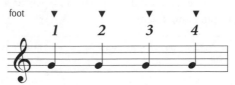

The quarter note: one beat in ⁴₄.

The eighth note: half a beat in ⁴₄

There are two *eighth notes* in one quarter note. In 'Bah Bah Black Sheep' the words 'have you any' are eighth notes: There are two notes for each beat. You can count these eighth notes out loud in various ways. Here are some examples:

An eighth note lasts half a beat in ⁴₄.

Sixteenth note: a quarter beat in ⁴₄

There are four *sixteenth notes* to one beat. Sixteenth notes sound twice as fast as eighth notes. Here are some ways to count them:

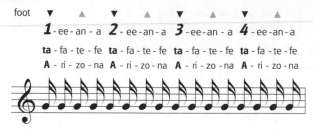

A sixteenth note lasts a quarter of a beat in $\frac{4}{4}$.

Heads, stems, and flags

How long a note lasts is referred to as its *note value*. The note's looks show you its note value. Every note is built up out of one, two, or three parts: an open or a closed head, a stem, and a flag.

the note	its name	its parts	lasts in (in $\frac{4}{4}$)
o	whole note	open head	four beats
♩	half note	open head and stem	two beats
♩	quarter note	closed head and stem	one beat
♪	eighth note	closed head, stem, and flag	half a beat
♪	sixteenth note	closed head, stem, and two flags	quarter beat

BARS AND TIME SIGNATURES

The bars or measures in a piece of music are divided by vertical lines: the *bar lines*.

Time signature

The number of beats per bar is always indicated at the beginning. 'Bah Bah Black Sheep' begins with $\frac{4}{4}$, pronounced as *four-four*. This is the *time signature*, and it tells you how long each bar is in a piece. This particular time signature,

$\frac{4}{4}$, is very common in Western music. It's so common, in fact, that it's also known as *common time*.

Four-four bar

In a piece in $\frac{4}{4}$, each bar lasts as long as four quarter notes. So it may contain four quarter notes, but also one whole note, or two quarter notes and a half note, and so on, as long as it all adds up to $4/4$. An example? A half note + a quarter note + two eighth notes fill up one $\frac{4}{4}$ bar. It's just a matter of basic math: $\frac{1}{2} + \frac{1}{4} + \frac{2}{8} = \frac{4}{4}$.

Upper number

The upper number in the time signature tells you how many beats there are in each bar. In a piece in $\frac{4}{4}$ there are four beats per bar.

Lower number and counting unit

The lower number indicates which note lasts *one* beat. In $\frac{4}{4}$, that's a quarter note: $\frac{1}{4}+\frac{1}{4}+\frac{1}{4}+\frac{1}{4} = \frac{4}{4}$. This implies that you count the piece in quarter notes: The quarter note is the *counting unit*.

Three-four

'My Bonnie Lies Over the Ocean' doesn't have four, but three quarter notes to every bar. Its time signature is $\frac{3}{4}$, or *three-four*, sometimes known as *waltz time*.

My   Bon - nie   lies   o - ver   the

'My Bonnie': three beats per bar.

Two or five

There are more time signatures than just $\frac{4}{4}$ and $\frac{3}{4}$. For example, time signatures with two beats per bar, such as $\frac{2}{4}$; (*e.g.*, 'Twinkle, Twinkle') or five beats per bar, such as $\frac{5}{4}$.

Another counting unit

Likewise, there are time signatures based on another counting unit; usually the eighth note. In $\frac{3}{8}$ there are three eighth notes in every bar. There's more about time signatures in Chapter 16.

C and ¢

Instead of ⁴⁄₄, the symbol **C** is used quite often: It's the C of *common time*. The symbol **¢** indicates a ²⁄₂ time signature, which is also known as *cut common time* or *alla breve*. In ²⁄₂, the half note is the counting unit; a half note equals one beat.

Triple time

A piece in *triple time* or *triple meter*, or simply *in three*, has three beats per bar (*e.g.*, ³⁄₄ or ³⁄₈).

BEAMS

Sequences of eighth, sixteenth, and shorter notes can be made easier to read if their individual flags are replaced by *beams*.

Individual notes make this melody hard to read.

The same melody: Beams group the notes and make them easier to read.

Beam = flag

A beam has the same value as a flag. An eighth note has one flag, so eighth notes are joined by a single beam. Sixteenth notes have two flags, so they're joined with a double beam.

One beat

A group of notes joined by a single or a multiple beam always represents the value of one beat, as shown in the example above: In ⁴⁄₄, beams join groups of two eighth notes, or four sixteenth notes. The first note of each group always falls on the beat, again making the music easier to read than it would be with individual notes.

One whole note, two half notes, four quarter notes, eight eighth notes, sixteen sixteenth notes: They all last four beats in $\frac{4}{4}$, filling up one bar.

Single and double beams
Single and double beams can be combined. In the examples below, each grouping has two sixteenths and one eighth note. This adds up to the value of one quarter note: $\frac{2}{16} + \frac{1}{8} = \frac{2}{4}$.

Combining single and double beams.

Fewer beams for singers
Music for singers often is written with fewer beams, as it can be impossible to arrange the lyrics underneath groups of notes.

Even shorter notes
The shortest note you have come across so far is the sixteenth, but there are also thirty-second notes and even shorter notes.

Sixty-four notes: sixteen notes equaling one quarter note.

RESTS

Each of the preceding examples assigns one or more notes to every beat. However, there's more to music than notes. The *rests* are just as important – silence, next to sound. A rest means you actually stop playing for a moment. Just like notes, there are whole, half, quarter, and shorter rests.

Rectangles and tags

In $\frac{4}{4}$, a *whole rest* lasts four beats, just like a whole note. The whole rest looks like a small solid rectangle hanging from the fourth line on the staff, counting from below. The *half-note rest* is a similar rectangle sitting on the third line. The *quarter-note rest* is a very special sign. The shorter rests, starting with the *eighth-note rest*, get *tags*: the more tags, the shorter the rest.

the rest	its name	lasts as long as		beats in $\frac{4}{4}$
	whole rest		whole note	four beats
	half rest		half note	two beats
	quarter rest		quarter note	one beat
	eighth rest		eighth note	half a beat
	sixteenth rest		sixteenth note	quarter beat

The rests in $\frac{4}{4}$.

Multiple bars

If you're supposed to keep quiet for a large number of bars, you'll see a special symbol with the exact number of bars specified above it.

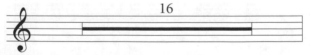

A sixteen-bar rest.

DOTS AND TIES

So far you've seen symbols that represent certain lengths for notes and rests: four beats, two beats, one beat, and so on. But there are also notes of other lengths – a beat-and-a-half, for example, or three beats. There are two ways to write such notes: with *dots* and with *ties*.

Dots

Notes can be made longer by adding a dot. A note followed by a dot is 1.5 times its original length. These dots are known as *augmentation dots*.

Two + one = three   Tipcode MOP-011

In $\frac{4}{4}$, a half note with a dot lasts 1.5 x two beats = three beats. A *dotted* quarter note lasts a beat and-a-half. And so on.

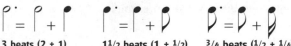

3 beats (2 + 1)   **1¹/2 beats (1 + ¹/2)**   **3/4 beats (1/2 + 1/4)**

Adding a dot makes a note last 1.5 times as long.

Dotted quarter notes and dotted half note.

Two dots and dotted rests

Notes can have two dots too, the second dot referring to the first one: in $\frac{4}{4}$, a double-dotted half note lasts 2 + 1 + ½ = three-and-a-half beats. Rests can be dotted and double-dotted as well.

$$\xi^{\cdot} = \xi + \gamma \qquad\qquad \gamma^{\cdot} = \gamma + \gamma$$

In $\frac{4}{4}$, a dotted quarter note rest lasts a beat-and-a-half. A dotted eighth note rest lasts three sixteenths.

Ties   Tipcode MOP-012

A *tie* extends a note by joining it to another note of the same pitch. If two notes are joined by a tie, the second note is simply held on, instead of being played separately.

1¹/₂ beats 2¹/₂ beats 1 beat   4¹/₂ beats

Ties join notes.   tie

Dots or ties?

Some feel that dotted notes are easier to read then tied notes, but ties allow for a few things that dots don't. Two examples: First, ties can make a note last into the following bar. Dots can't. Second, ties allow for notes that last, say, two-and-a-half beats, as shown above. Dots offer less options.

TRIPLETS AND OTHER –PLETS

As you have seen, each note can be divided into two, four, eight, or more shorter notes. But you can also divide notes into three or five, for example.

Triplets   Tipcode MOP-013

If you divide a quarter note into two, you get two eighth notes. When you divide it into three, you get a *triplet* made up of three eighth notes, known as an *eighth-note triplet.* Triplets are marked with the number 3 above or below the three notes, sometimes with a square bracket or a curved line.

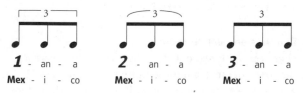

Two ways to count eighth-note triplets, and three ways to write them.

Sixteenth-note triplets

Sixteenth-note triplets are formed by dividing eighth notes into three: You have to play three sixteenths in the time it would normally take to play two.

An eighth note followed by a sixteenth-note triplet, and vice versa.

Quarter-note triplets   Tipcode MOP-014

A quarter-note triplet is what you get if a half note is divided into three. It takes time to learn to play quarter-note triplets, since you have to play three notes while counting two beats.

Not always all three

You don't always play all three notes of a triplet, of course. Below are some eighth-note triplets with one note missing:

Mex – i – **co**

Mex – **i** – co

Mex – **i** – **co**

Two notes as a single note

Sometimes two notes in a triplet (usually the first and second) are played as a single note. In this case you only hear two notes but there's no rest in between. This can be written in two ways:

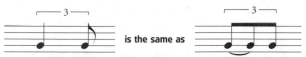

Two ways to indicate a triplet with the first two notes played as a single note.

Sextuplets   Tipcode MOP-015

Notes can also be divided into six: the *sextuplet*.

A quarter note divided into six: a sixteenth-note sextuplet.

DadadaDadada

Two sixteenth-note triplets seem very similar to a sextuplet, but there *is* a difference. Two sixteenth-note triplets are usually felt as two groups of three (DadadaDadada). A sextuplet usually feels more like three groups of two (DadaDadaDada) or one group of six (Dadadadadada).

Da – da – da   Da – da – da

Da – da   Da – da   Da – da

The difference: two sixteenth-note triplets and a sextuplet.

Five or seven

Tipcode MOP-016

It may take a little while to get used to the slightly different feel of triplets and sextuplets, but in fact they're very common. Other subdivisions, such as the *quintuplet* (a note divided into five) and the *septuplet* (divided into seven) are much less common in Western music.

Quintuplet and septuplet.

PICKUP

A measure or bar is always completely full. For example, each bar in a ⁴⁄₄ piece contains a combination of notes and rests that add up to the same value as four quarter notes.

Pickup

There is one exception to this rule: The very first bar of a piece may be shorter. Many compositions begin with an 'incomplete' first bar. This is called a *pickup* or *upbeat*. Classical musicians sometimes call it an *anacrusis*.

'My Bonnie Lies Over the Ocean' begins with a pickup. 'My' is the pickup, on the third beat of the incomplete first bar; 'Bonnie' starts on one in the second bar.

The final bar

If there's an incomplete first bar, there's often an incomplete final bar too, adding up to one full bar: If a piece in ⁴⁄₄ starts with a one-beat pickup, the final bar will often have three beats.

Pickup in a complete bar

Pickups may also appear in the context of a complete bar: If there's a quarter-note pickup, for example, it is preceded by a half-note rest and a quarter-note rest.

4. SHARPS AND FLATS

The natural or white notes discussed in Chapter 2 are just seven of the twelve notes in one octave. This chapter looks at the other five – the black notes – and explains sharps and flats.

The black notes are named in relation to the white notes: If a black note is a half step higher than a white note it's called a *sharp*; if a black note is a half step lower than a white note it's called a *flat*.

Twinkle, Twinkle

With the last two chapters in mind you can now read and play 'Twinkle, Twinkle.' Your ears will tell you if you've got it right.

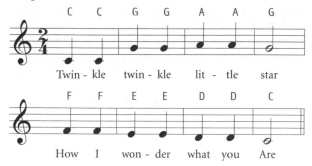

From C to C

'Twinkle, Twinkle' begins with two Cs. For the next two notes (G), you move five white keys up. From there, you move up one more white key (A), and than you move down the white notes, key by key, ending up again on C.

From F to F
Tipcode MOP-017

If every piece of music began and ended on C, life would be pretty monotonous. So why not begin 'Twinkle, Twinkle' on another note – on F, for example. If you do so and follow the same route as if you'd started in C, you'll hear that something goes wrong. The B, on the words 'how I,' sounds too high.

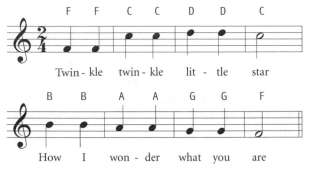

'Twinkle, Twinkle' starting on F. The Bs on 'How I' sound too high.

Lowering a note

The solution is to lower the B by a half step. On a keyboard you play this lowered B by hitting the black key just to the left of it.

Flats
Tipcode MOP-018

The lowered B is indicated with a *flat* (♭). To play a flatted note on a keyboard instrument, you simply move one black or white key to the left. That note sounds a half step lower. Here is 'Twinkle, Twinkle,' starting on F, now with a B♭ (pronounced as *B-flat*) to make it sound right.

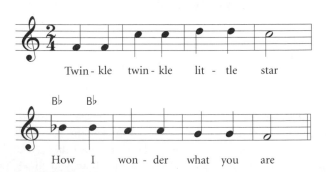

'Twinkle, Twinkle' starting on F. The flat turns both Bs into B♭s.

The other flats

The other natural notes can be lowered in exactly the same way.

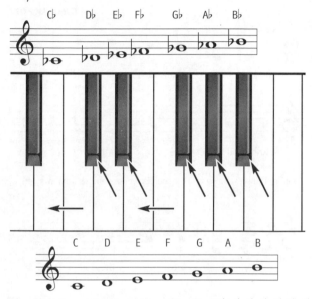

The natural notes and the lowered naturals, or flats: C♭, D♭, E♭, F♭, G♭, A♭, B♭.

Belly and head

On the staff, the 'belly' of each flat symbol clearly shows which note it refers to: The belly is at the same line or space as the head of that note.

Flats and white keys

Most lowered naturals are played on black keys. The naturals C and F are rarely lowered. But when they are, you play these lowered notes on white keys: As you can see above, C♭ uses the same key as B, and F♭ is played on the key that's commonly known as E.

SOUNDS FLAT? USE A SHARP!

If you would begin 'Twinkle, Twinkle' on a D and use white keys only, you'd hear that the F on the word 'wonder' sounds too low.

Too low

The solution is to raise the F a half step. On a keyboard

you simply play the black note to the right of the F. On paper this raised note is indicated as F♯, pronounced *F-sharp*.

Tipcode MOP-022

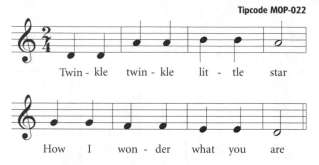

'Twinkle, Twinkle' starting on D. It sounds too low on the word 'wonder'.

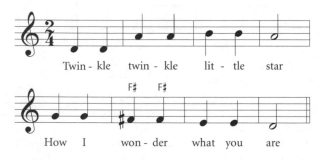

'Twinkle, Twinkle' starting on D. The sharp turns the Fs into F♯s.

Which one?

Each sharp clearly indicates the note you should raise: The middle of each sharp on a staff is at the same line or space as the note it refers to.

E♯ and B♯

Most raised naturals are played on the black keys. The rare E♯ and B♯ are played on white keys instead: B♯ is played on the C-key, and the E♯ corresponds with the white F-key.

ACCIDENTALS AND KEY SIGNATURES

Sharps and flats are *chromatic signs*. You may find chromatic signs in one or more bars of a piece, as well as at the very beginning, next to the clef.

One bar

When there is a sharp or a flat in a bar, anywhere in a piece of music, it is only valid for that same bar. In 'Twinkle, Twinkle' on D, one sharp raises both Fs in that bar.

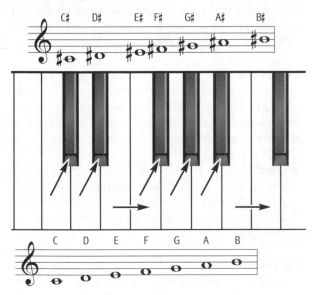

The raised naturals, or sharps.

Accidentals

When used this way, sharps and flats are called *accidentals*. An accidental applies to the notes at the same line or space within the same bar. If there's an accidental for the note Middle C in a bar, it applies to the following Middle Cs in that bar, but not for a higher or a lower C.

One exception

If a note with an accidental is tied over a bar line, the accidental applies to both bits of the tied note. It's no longer valid when that note has ended: In the example below, the sharp needs to be repeated in the second bar.

An accidental applies throughout a tied note, but not to the rest of the next bar.

31

Next to the clef

You'll often see one or more sharps or flats at the very beginning of a piece, next to the clef. These sharps or flats apply to the whole piece and to every octave. If there's one flat next to the clef, every B in the piece should be lowered to B♭, not just the ones at the same line or space as the symbol.

Key signature

The sharps or flats at the clef don't just tell you which notes to lower or to raise: They also indicate the *key signature* of the piece, or what *key* a piece is in. There's more information on keys and key signatures in Chapters 10 to 14.

Every staff

In classical notation, the clef(s) and the key signature are usually repeated at the beginning of every staff. Non-classical composers and arrangers often print it only once, at the beginning of the piece.

Which notes   Tipcode MOP-019

A key signature can contain one, two, three, or more sharps or flats – or none, if the piece is in the key of C. Each sharp or flat clearly indicates the note it refers to. You can also tell which notes to lower or to raise by looking at the number of flats or sharps: Sharps and flats always appear in a fixed order.

C♯   F♯   C♯   F♯

Key signature with two sharps: Every C and F is raised.

Always

If there's just one sharp, it always raises each F to F♯. If there are two sharps in the key signature, you also raise each C to C♯. Three sharps raise each F, C, and G. This order continues as shown on the opposite page. The seventh sharp raises each B to B♯.

Seven flats

In a piece with one flat, every B turns into a B♭. Two flats

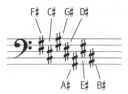

All sharps in the bass and treble clefs.

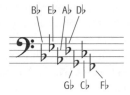

All flats in the bass and treble clefs.

flatten every B and E. Again, the order continues, as shown above. The seventh flat lowers F to F♭.

Memorize

It's good to memorize these orders, at least up to three or four flats and sharps. (Key signatures with more flats or sharps are rare.) Then, if you see a piece in three flats, for example, you'll know right away that you're supposed to lower all Bs, Es and As.

System

The fixed orders of flats and sharps are not coincidental. There's a system behind it. Chapter 11 tells you all about it.

Natural signs   Tipcode MOP-020

Flats and sharps can be suspended within a single bar by the *natural sign* (♮).

Natural sign, turning the key signature's B♭ into B.

Accidentals too

A key signature at the beginning of a piece doesn't mean you won't run into one or more accidentals too, raising or lowering individual notes.

33

Reminder

Sometimes sharps, flats, and natural signs are given as reminders, helping to prevent you from hitting the wrong note. These *reminder accidentals* often appear in parentheses.

ONE NOTE, TWO NAMES

If you take one more look at the two keyboard illustrations on the previous pages, you'll see that keys can actually have two names. The middle key in the group of the three black ones is an A♭, if it happens to be a lowered A. But it can also be a G♯, if it happens to be a raised G in another song.

Enharmonic notes

Two notes that sound the same, such as A♭ and G♯, are said to be *enharmonic equivalents*: They have different names, but you play them on the same key on a piano, you use the same fingering on a wind instrument, or you stop a string at the same fret on a guitar. You'll find other examples of enharmonic notes in the example below. They also include 'white' notes, of course: B♯ and C are enharmonic, for example, and F♭ and E too.

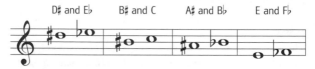

Enharmonic equivalents.

The key signature

Whether a certain note is a G♯ or an A♭ depends, for one thing, on the key signature, which determines whether notes should be raised or lowered in a piece. This was illustrated by starting 'Twinkle, Twinkle' on different notes, in the beginning of this chapter. Want to know more? Then check out Chapter 10.

Going up, going down

In choosing whether to use an accidental sharp or an accidental flat, the direction of the melody is important: If the melody goes up, the composer is likely to use a sharp sign. When the direction is downward, a flat will be used.

Stepping stone
Tipcode MOP-021

Here's an example. In the first bar, the direction of the melody is upward, and the G♯ is a stepping stone to the A. In the second bar, the direction is downward, and the enharmonic A♭ (which sound the same as the G♯) leads down to the G.

The G♯ and the A♭: same pitch, different name, different effect.

DOUBLE SHARPS AND FLATS

Doubly raised and lowered notes are quite rare, but you may come across them. The double flat (♭♭) lowers the natural note by two half steps. The note G preceded by a double-flat is called a *G double-flat*, and on a keyboard you play it using the F-key.

Double sharp

The double-sharp has its own symbol: 𝄪. It raises a note two half steps. The note G preceded by a double-sharp sign is a *G double-sharp*, equaling an A on a keyboard.

Why not an A

Why not simply write an A instead of a G𝄪? For the same reason that a G♯ sounds like an A♭, but is, in effect, a different note: Within the music as written, it functions as either a raised G or a lowered A. Double sharps and flats make reading music quite complicated – unnecessarily complicated, according to many composers – so it's not that unusual to put an A on paper when it's actually supposed to be a G𝄪 or a B♭♭.

5. LOUD AND SOFT

If you play every single note at the same volume, you'll sound more like a machine than a musician. In most styles of music changes in volume – the dynamics – are very important.

In musical terms, variations in volume are called *dynamics*. On paper, *dynamic markings* indicate how loudly or softly you should play. Dynamics are usually indicated by Italian words or their abbreviations. These are the standard dynamic markings:

	Meaning	Indicating
ppp	pianisissimo	very, very soft
pp	pianissimo	very soft
p	piano	soft
mp	mezzo piano	moderately soft
mf	mezzo forte	moderately loud
f	forte	loud; strong
ff	fortissimo	very loud; very strong
fff	fortisissimo	very, very loud; very, very strong

As loud as possible

Occasionally, you may come across dynamic markings with four or even more letters (such as *ffff* or *pppp*), which basically tell you to play as loud or as soft as possible. Obviously, how much noise you actually make depends on your instrument. On a violin, *ff* generates less sound than on a snare drum. One more thing: *Mezzo piano* is only very slightly softer than *mezzo forte*.

Until the next

Dynamic markings are always under the first note they apply to. From that note onward you keep playing at the indicated volume until you come across the next dynamic marking.

Gradually

There are also dynamic markings that tell you to get gradually louder (*crescendo*) or softer (*decrescendo*).

Crescendo

Crescendo (Italian for 'growing') tells you to get gradually louder over a number of notes or bars. The sign used for short crescendos clearly indicates this: It shows two diverging lines (————————) under notes or bars it applies to. A crescendo that's stretched over a larger number of bars is often indicated by the word 'crescendo,' or the abbreviation *cresc.*, followed by a dotted line that shows how long the change in volume should last.

Decrescendo – getting softer

A short *decrescendo* is indicated by two converging lines (————————). For long decrescendos, you'll find the full word or its abbreviation *decresc.* or *decr.*, followed by a dotted line. *Diminuendo* (*dim.*) is another word for decrescendo.

Reading ahead

Tipcode MOP-023

How much louder or softer you should get is indicated by a dynamic marking at the end of the (de)crescendo – so do read ahead.

f *p* ——————————— *f*

A short crescendo, from piano to forte.

Sudden changes

A note or chord marked *fp* (meaning *fortepiano*) should start with a loud 'burst' but then quickly drop in volume. A *sforzando* (*sfz* or *sf*) also tells you to play with sudden extra force, but with this marking the extra volume should last for the whole note or chord. These markings are often followed by a *crescendo*.

CHAPTER 5

Per note

Because they apply to one note or chord only, *fortepiano* and *sforzando* are really types of accents. There's more about accents in Chapter 7, *Articulation*.

English

In non-classical music, dynamics are often indicated in English. These terms, which have not been standardized, are often more descriptive than simply 'loud' or 'soft'. A dynamic marking such as 'screaming,' for instance, tells you to make your instrument scream – and that's more than just playing it really loudly.

6. FAST AND SLOW

There are two main ways of indicating the speed or tempo of a piece of music – with numbers or Italian terms. Additionally, there are all sorts of words that indicate *how* a piece should be played.

The most precise way of indicating the tempo of a piece is by stating the number of *beats per minute* (BPM). You will often find this indication at the top of the piece. It shows a note (usually the counting unit) and a number, such as (♩ = **120**). This example indicates that there should be 120 quarter notes in a minute (2 per second!).

March time
This tempo is about the same as the number of steps you take per minute at a brisk walk: It's commonly known as *march time*.

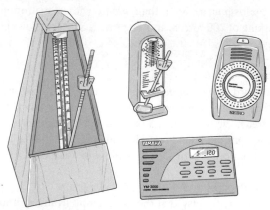

Two mechanical metronomes and two electronic ones.

Metronome

Tipcode MOP-024

You can set the number of beats per minute on a *metronome*, a device that will play that tempo with steady ticks or beeps. Most metronomes have a range of 40 to 208 beats per minute. Music written any slower than 40 BPM is extremely rare. For really fast pieces, you simply halve the metronome indication. If the tempo is 240 ((♩= **240**), you set the metronome to 120.

Italian

The other way to indicate tempo is with Italian words. Most metronomes show the common Italian tempo markings and how they relate to BPM. These are the main markings:

Italian	Translation	Metronome Marking
Largo	very slow	♩ = **40-60**
Adagio	slow	♩ = **66-76**
Andante	walking, relaxed tempo	♩ = **76-108**
Moderato	medium tempo	♩ = **108-120**
Allegro	fast	♩ = **120-168**
Presto	very fast	♩ = **168-200**

Prestissimo and larghetto

These tempo markings and other Italian terms often appear with different endings or suffixes. The suffix -*issimo*, for instance, means 'more than,' while -*etto* stands for 'less than'. So *prestissimo* is faster than *presto*, with a metronome marking of 200 to 208, and *larghetto* is a bit less slow than *largo*.

Rubato

The word *rubato* appears mainly in tranquil pieces. It indicates that you're free to play a few notes a bit faster, then to stretch the tempo just a bit, and so on. The expression stems from the Italian word for robbing: You 'steal' a little time from one bar or note and add it to another.

Tempo changes

Most pieces are played at the same tempo from beginning to end. While in most cases it's up to the drummer or the conductor to keep that tempo steady, it is a good idea to use a metronome when practicing, from time to time – so you can learn to keep your time in your own hands. In some pieces the tempo does change, however. One of the most common examples is that you need to slow down towards the end, in the last few bars.

Italian words

Gradual tempo changes are usually marked with Italian words:

- *Accelerando* (as in a car's accelerator) and *stringendo* (*string.*; urgently) indicate that the tempo should increase.
- If you have to slow down, you'll read *ritenuto* (*rit.* or *riten.*), *rallentando* (*rall.*), or *ritardando* (*ritard.*).
- *Allargando* means 'broadening out,' and it can be interpreted as indicating a crescendo as well as a decrease in speed.
- *A Tempo* or *Tempo I^o* ('tempo primo') tells you should return to the original tempo.

Gradually

Just as with gradual changes of volume, the words *poco a poco* (bit by bit) may be added if the change should be *very* gradual.

Ad libitum

Ad libitum or *ad lib.* means 'at liberty,' implying that how you play a passage or a piece of music is up to you. It often refers to the tempo, but it may also have another, or a much broader meaning. An example: *8va ad lib.* means you may consider playing that section an octave higher, should you feel like it.

English

Of course, English can be used to indicate the tempo as well, ranging from the basic 'fast' to more musical expressions such as *ballad* or *up tempo*.

M.M.

A final note: Metronome markings sometimes include the abbreviation M.M. This stands for Maelzel's Metronome. In the early nineteenth century, Maelzel improved and patented the metronome, which was invented by a Dutchman by the name of Winkel.

TEMPOS AND MOODS

If you write a song to tell the world you just won the lottery, you are likely to pick a pretty high tempo – and vice versa. The tempo often reflects the mood of a piece of music. It doesn't say everything, though. If you can play, you can make a piece feel heavy, or light; or make it sound exciting or boring, all at one tempo.

Feeling

There are many words that are used to indicate the mood or feeling that the composer had in mind. Apart from the following Italian words, you can come across indications in other languages as well:

agitato	agitated
con brio	with brilliance
con fuoco	with fire
con spirito	with spirit or vigor
dolce	sweetly, lovely
tranquillo	calmly, easy, tranquil
vivace	lively

Very, more, or less

The words in the following list are often combined with terms already mentioned:

assai	quite, rather
molto	very
meno	less
(ma) non troppo	(but) not too much
più	more
un poco	a little, a bit
e	and

A mouthful

So *un poco più presto* tells you to start playing a little faster. And *poco a poco stringendo e crescendo ma non troppo?* Gradually get a little faster and a bit louder as well, but please, don't overdo it.

7. ARTICULATION

Just as with words, you can 'pronounce' or articulate notes in different ways. The way notes should be articulated is indicated by a variety of symbols printed above or below the note(s).

Tipcode MOP-025

The best known articulation sign is the *accent*: a horizontal 'V' above or below a note, telling you to emphasize it by playing it a little louder.

Accented notes.

Marcato

An upside-down 'V' means *marcato* ('marked' or 'stressed'). Notes with this sign should be played louder, and often just a bit shorter as well. If there is a dot inside the sign, the notes have to be even shorter. You may also find the word *marcato* indicating a group of notes or bars that should be played this way.

Marcato: stressed.

Staccato Tipcode MOP-026

Notes with a dot above or below them are to be played *staccato*: very short and clipped. Remember though, a *staccato* quarter note sounds shorter than a regular quarter note, but the note value doesn't change: It takes up as much time in the music. Sometimes, instead of every note having a dot, a passage is marked with the word *staccato*.

Staccato: short notes.

Staccatissimo

If there's a small triangle, instead of a dot, the notes should be played *staccatissimo*: even shorter than *staccato*.

Staccatissimo: even shorter notes.

Legato
Tipcode MOP-027

Legato (literally 'bound') is the opposite of *staccato*. When music is played *legato*, the notes are held on slightly longer than usual so there is no gap between them. A legato is marked with a *slur*: a curved line that binds notes together into groups. If you're a string player, you should play such groups in a single bowing action. Horn players play them with one breath.

Legato: The notes are smoothly bound together.

Phrase mark
Tipcode MOP-028

The *phrase mark* looks very similar to a legato slur, but has a different meaning. It joins a larger number of notes together in a phrase, just like words. And that's how you play them: as a phrase. Of course you may find other markings under a phrase mark, such as the *legato* slurs and the accents in the following example.

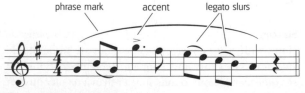

Phrase mark: to be played like a phrase.

Tenuto

You can also stress a note by making it slightly longer. This is known as an *agogic accent*. To emphasize a note in a sequence of notes of the same duration, it can be given a *tenuto* mark: a dash under the note, indicating that it should be slightly extended.

Portato

For string players, similar dashes indicate a number of notes that should be played by moving the bow in one direction only – up or down. This is known as *portato*; it can also be indicated with a combination of a slur and dots below the notes.

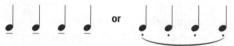

Tenuto: slightly extend the marked notes.

Simile

The word similar stems from the Italian word *simile*. *Simile* tells you to continue a certain way of playing. Printed after a few staccato notes, for instance, it means that all the notes that follow are to be played *staccato* too.

Fermata

A *fermata* is a note or chord that is sustained until the conductor, the band leader, or the drummer puts an end to it – or, if you're playing solo, until you are done with it. In most cases the note is played longer than the note value indicates. You usually find a fermata or pause at the end of a piece. It's indicated by a dot within a curved line.

Fermata: for as long as it lasts...

Pizzicato and arpeggio Tipcode MOP-029

Of course, there are lots of other ways to indicate how notes should be played. Some of them you'll only find in parts for a specific instrument or a group of instruments. *Pizzicato*, for example, tells violinists, cellists, and other string instrument players to pluck the strings, rather than to bow them. *Arpeggios* are found in parts for musicians who can play chords (*e.g.*, pianists and guitarists). It tells you to 'spread' a chord out, introducing the notes one by one – as if they're played on a harp. Other articulation markings are used only in specific styles.

JAZZ

Some examples of articulation markings in jazz are the scoop, the du-wah, and ghost notes. These markings are sometimes referred to as ornaments. There's more about ornaments in the next chapter.

Scoop

A *scoop* tells you to briefly bend the pitch of a note downward, not more than a half step. Scoops are most commonly found in sax parts.

A scoop.

Du and wah

The *du-wah* is used mainly by brass players. The 'du' (a plus sign above the note) tells you to smother the sound putting your hand or a plunger (a type of mute) in front of the bell of the instrument. The 'wah' (a small circle) tells you to open up the bell again. Harmonica players du-wah with their hands, and a guitarist's *wah-wah* pedal produces a similar effect.

Smothered and open: du-wah du-wah.

Ghost notes

A *ghost note* is a dead-sounding, 'swallowed' note with a hardly definable pitch. Every instrument has its specific techniques for making these notes. Wind players use their tongue, guitarists damp the string they're playing, and so on. Drummers play ghost notes as soft taps on the snare drum, between the other beats.

Ghost note: dead-sounding.

8. ORNAMENTS

In music, ornaments are decorative notes that embellish the main notes. This chapter introduces the most common ones, from trills to turns, and shows how to play them. The exact rhythm of each, though, can change depending on tempo and taste.

Tipcode MOP-030

There are dozens of ornaments, divided in a few large families. The *shake* family, for example, includes the trill, the mordent, and the vibrato, among others; the ornaments in the *appoggiatura* family all have an accessory note added to the main note; the *division* family divides a note into a few shorter ones.

Trill

Perhaps the best-known ornament is the *trill*, played by rapidly alternating between the *main* or *principal note* and the next higher note in the key signature, called the *upper note*. A trill can begin either on the principal note or on the upper note.

Trill.

Mordent

There are two mini-trills, called *mordents*. The regular or *lower mordent* is a very rapid trill with the note one step below. It is also known as *open shake* or *beat*.

47

Written: Played:

Mordent: short trill to the lower note.

Inverted mordent

The *inverted* or *upper mordent* indicates a similar trill with the note one step up. This mordent is also known as a *Prall trill*. The only visible difference between the symbols for the lower and the upper mordent is that the lower mordent has a small vertical line.

Written: Played:

Upper or inverted mordent: short trill to the upper note.

Sharps, flats, and trills

Trills and mordents are played on the note above or below the principal note in the key signature that you're in – sharps and flats remain valid. If the figure is to include a note that's not in the key signature, a flat, sharp, or natural sign will make this clear.

Written: Played:

Mordent with a temporarily lowered E (E♭).

Tremolo

A *tremolo* is usually a quick repetition of one note. On brass wind instruments you can play a tremolo on one note by making a r-r-rolling 'r' with your tongue. In classical music this is called *flutter tonguing* or – in German – *Flatterzunge*; jazz musicians speak of *growling*.

Written: Played:

Tremolo on one note.

Vibrato

A *vibrato* is a repeated, very slight pitch fluctuation, usually less than half a step. On fretted instruments (*e.g.*, guitars) and string instruments, you rock the finger that stops the string. Wind players use their *embouchure* (the muscles in and around the mouth) and air stream control.

No symbol

You may find the word *vibrato* (*vib.*, *vibr.*) under a note, but the use of vibrato is commonly up to the player or the conductor – unless the composer specifies *non-vibr.* Occasionally, the term vibrato is used to indicate a fluctuation of the intensity or volume.

Vibrato or tremolo?

Vibrato and *tremolo* often get mixed up. The handle you see on many electric guitars, for example, is often called the *tremolo arm*, but it can't be used to play a tremolo. It *can* be used to play a vibrato (quickly move the handle up and down, over a very small distance) or a *pitch bend*, by moving the handle once, over a larger distance.

Short appoggiatura

A *grace note* or *appoggiatura* is an ornamental note that precedes the main note, indicated by a tiny eighth note with a slash. You can play it just before the beat on which the main note falls, or on the beat, followed by the main note.

Written: Played:

Grace note: a short note preceding the principal note.

Turn

A *turn* or *gruppetto* ('division') tells you to play around the principal note. The symbol clearly shows what it's supposed to sound like.

Written: Played:

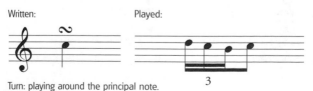

Turn: playing around the principal note.

3

The turn between two notes

You may also come across turn symbols between two notes. This ornament joins up the notes, as it were.

Written: Played:

Three extra notes between two main notes.

Glissando

In a *glissando* you slide from one note to another. The way to play it varies per instrument. On a trombone you use the slide, of course; on a keyboard instrument you sweep your fingertips over the keys; on fretted instruments and string instruments you slide your fingers over the strings. Many electronic keyboard instruments have a *pitch bend* control, allowing you to bend a note up or down. A *slide* can be seen as a very short glissando; it's actually an appoggiatura with two accessory notes.

Glissando: sliding from note to note.

Fall, lift, plop, and doit

A *glissando* always indicates a first and a last note. *Falls*, *lifts*, *plops*, and *doits* don't. Their symbols show you quite clearly how they should be played. The exact execution is up to you or your musical director.

Fall: Falling down from the note.

Lift: Move up from the note.

Plop: Falling into the note, from above.

Doit: a short upward bend of the note.

9. SECTION MARKINGS AND REPEAT SIGNS

Compositions usually consist of a number of different sections, such as the verses and choruses that make up most songs. Often, these sections repeat a number of times, or the song might skip backwards or forwards to a particular point. To save whole sections being written out more than once, there are a number of special markings that act like signposts, directing you around a piece of music.

Next to verses and choruses, there are plenty of other names to indicate the various parts of a piece of music. In a song, the word *intro* refers to the first section, before the music really gets going – which is usually when the vocals come in. The term *outro* is often used for the final section, when the singing has stopped. A *bridge* literally bridges two different sections.

Expositions and interludes

There are also a whole array of names for the sections of classical pieces, from *exposition* (an opening section) and *recapitulation* (a return to the opening), to *interlude* or *transition* (classical 'bridges').

Section markings

The various sections of a piece are often indicated by letters. These *section markings* are also known as *rehearsal marks*, as that's when they're often used: Instead of playing a piece from the top after every mistake, the conductor may suggest to 'take it from H,' for example. These markings are usually written in small boxes above the staff.

Bar numbers

A number placed above a bar line – on its own, in a circle or in a box – usually indicates the number of the following bar, counting from the beginning of the piece. Occasionally, numbers are used as section or rehearsal markings, instead of letters.

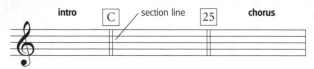

Names, letters, or numbers are used to identify the various parts of a piece.

Section lines

Sections are often marked by *section lines* (thin, double bar lines). They're also often used if there's a change of key signature.

Double bar line

The *double bar line* (a normal bar line followed by a thick one) indicates the end of a piece. It is also used in repeat signs, which are explained in the next section.

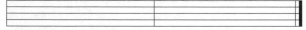

Double bar line: the end.

REPEAT SIGNS

Repeat signs tell you to repeat one or more bars, or a section of the piece.

One and two bars

The repeat sign for a single bar is a slash with a dot on either side. A similar symbol with two slashes tells you to repeat the two preceding bars.

Repeat the previous bar.   Repeat the previous two bars.

Repeating

A section that should be played twice is usually marked with two *repeat signs*, one on either end of the section. The illustration shows what they look like. When you reach the second sign (its two dots facing 'backward'), you go back to the first sign (its dots facing 'forward') and play again from there, repeating what you just played.

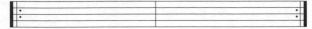

Repeat the bars between these two signs.

Just one

If you have to repeat the first section of a piece, there may be just one repeat sign (the 'second' one, its dots facing to the left. When you reach it, you go back to the beginning of the piece and play once more what you just played.

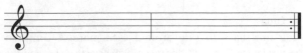

Repeat from the beginning.

First and second ending

Sometimes a repeated section ends differently the second time around. This is indicated with square brackets marked 1 and 2, as in the example below. You end the section the first time around by playing the bar or bars marked 1 (*first ending*). When you get to this point the second time, you skip to the bar or bars marked 2 (*second ending*).

Fourth ending

If you need to play a section three times with the first ending and then skip to the second ending, the first bracket will contain the numbers 1, 2, and 3, and there'll be a 4 in the second bracket.

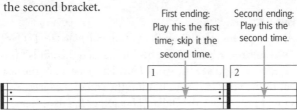

First ending:
Play this the first time; skip it the second time.

Second ending:
Play this the second time.

First and second ending.

SKIPPING AROUND

A variety of symbols, words and abbreviations is used to indicate that you have to skip from one part of a piece to another.

Da Capo

Da Capo (*D.C.*) means that you go back to the beginning of a piece and repeat everything you played so far. The intro shouldn't be included unless it is indicated that you should. When you reach D.C. the second time, ignore it and continue with the music that follows.

Dal Segno

Dal Segno (*D.S.*) means 'from the sign.' When you reach a D.S., you go back to the 𝄋 sign (the *segno*), which always precedes the D.S. You repeat the bars between the segno and the D.S. once, and ignore D.S. the second time you reach it.

Al Coda

You may have to skip around even more. A common example: *Da Capo Al Coda* means you have to go back to the beginning of the piece (D.C.), and play until you reach the coda sign 𝄌. This sign tells you to skip to the *coda*, which is a section at the end of the piece, marked with that word.

To the coda

Al coda is Italian for 'to the coda.' Instead of those exact words, you may also find the indication Al 𝄌.

Other combinations

Coda markings can be combined with other instructions. *Dal Segno al* 𝄌, for example, tells you to go back to the 𝄋 sign, play on until you reach the 𝄌 sign, and then skip to the coda.

Fine

Al Fine means 'to the end'. *Da Capo al Fine* (or *D.C. al Fine*) means go back to the beginning, and then finish the piece where you see the word *Fine*. This *Fine* is not the last bar of the printed music, but it *is* the end of the piece. You should pronounce the Italian *Fine* somewhat like 'Feenah'.

Example

Here's an example of a piece of music with various repeat and section markings.
1. Play the first seven bars plus the first ending (Section A, first time).

2. Repeat the first seven bars and play the second ending (Section A, second time).
3. Play Section B.
4. Go back to the beginning at *D.C. al Coda*.
5. From the Coda sign (Section A, seventh bar) you skip to the *Coda*.
6. The double bar line at the end of the coda is the end of the piece.

An AABA song with various repeat and section markings.

AABA

The form of this particular piece is referred to as AABA: You play the A section twice, followed by the bridge (B), and finally A again. If you sing the theme song from *The Flintstones*, you'll find it has the same form, just like many jazz standards and Broadway musical songs.

REPEATING NOTES AND CHORDS

Other signs tell you to repeat single chords, single notes, and pairs of alternating notes.

Repeating chords

If a chord is followed by a slash or series of slashes, then you should repeat the chord once for each slash.

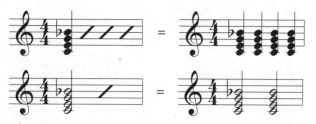

Repeat the chord once for each slash.

Repeating notes

A single note with one or more slashes tells you to repeat the note. The note itself tells you how long you should continue repeating the note; the number of slashes tells you what sort of notes to play, *e.g.*, eighth or sixteenth notes.

Different pitch

A repetition of two notes of different pitch can be indicated in a similar way.

10. MAJOR AND MINOR

If you play all the natural notes from C to C, you're playing a scale: C, D, E, F, G, A, B, C. Do the same from A to A, and you will hear a scale which clearly sounds different. Most compositions are based on the notes belonging to one particular scale. The name of that scale is referred to as the key. This chapter deals with the two most important scales: major and minor.

It's not essential to know about scales and keys in order to read music – but it *does* help you to understand what you're playing, instead of just playing the notes one by one, with no sense of their function in the context of the music. It definitely makes improvising and writing your own music a lot easier too.

In a row

Pick any tune and arrange all its notes in a row, from low to high. What you will end up with is a scale, or part of a scale. 'Twinkle, Twinkle,' for example, is made up of the

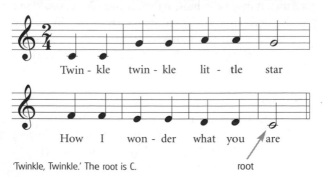

Twin - kle twin - kle lit - tle star

How I won - der what you are

'Twinkle, Twinkle.' The root is C.   root notes C, G, A, G, F, E, D, C. Arranged from low to high (C, D, E, F, G, A), these are the first six notes of a scale.

Root

If you sing 'Twinkle, Twinkle' and stop at the words 'what you,' it probably feels like your ending it in mid-flight – there's got to be more to come. The note you're missing is the *root note* or, simply, *root*. With this last note you go back, so to speak, to where it all started: the root. The root is usually the first note of the scale that's been used for the piece.

Coming home

Most pieces end on the root of the scale in which they are written. Another term for root, clearly indicating this function, is *home note*. It's also known as the *tonic* or the *key note*.

The scale of C

'Twinkle, Twinkle,' in the version above, is made up of the first six notes of the scale of C. To complete the scale, just add the B and a second C: What you get is C, D, E, F, G, A, B, C. On a keyboard, you'll see that it is made up of natural (white) notes only.

Whole steps and half steps

If you go from one white key to the next on a keyboard, you play a mixture of whole and half steps. From C to D and from D to E are whole steps. From E to F is a half step.

The difference

The difference between whole and half steps is easier to see than it may be to hear, at first. If you take a closer look at the keyboard, you'll see that there is no black key between E and F. This shows that the step from one to the other is a half step. From B to C (no black key in between) is a half step too.

Major scale

The scale above consists of seven steps. There are five whole steps (W) and two half steps (H), in the following order: W, W, H, W, W, W, H. Any scale whose steps are arranged in this order is a *major scale*.

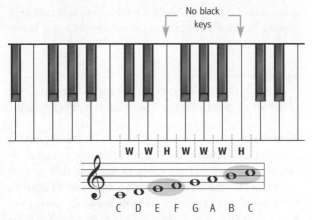

The scale of C. The two half steps are from E to F, and from B to C.

Different order, different sound

If you change the order of whole and half steps, you'll end up with a different scale; a scale with a different character due to the altered order of whole and half steps.

A circle

Drawing these steps in a circle shows these differences. First follow the steps in the circle starting on C (the root),

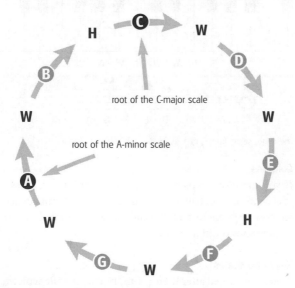

The roots of the C-major and A-minor scales. Follow the arrows and you will see the different orders of the steps for these scales.

going round clockwise. You'll see the whole and half steps coming by in the order mentioned above: It's a major scale.

Another note

If you start on another note, you'll get a different order of the whole and half steps. The result is a different scale.

Minor scale

Tipcode MOP-031

If you have a keyboard instrument at hand, you can easily hear that difference. First, listen to the scale that you get when you play the white keys from C to the next higher C. Then move a little to the left and play the white notes from A to the next higher A. The second scale sounds a little lower, but it also sounds a bit sadder or darker than the major scale. This scale is known as the *minor scale*. You play the same white keys, but the scale sounds different because the order of whole and half steps is different: W, H, W, W, H, W, W.

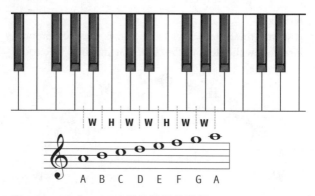

The minor scale, from A to A: W, H, W, W, H, W, W.

Columns

If you draw the steps of the major and minor scales as a row of whole and half-sized columns, you will immediately see how different they look – and things that look different, usually sound different too.

Keys and scales

Scales are named after their root. The major scale with the root C is the *C-major scale*. A piece of music that uses these notes is in the *key of C-major*.

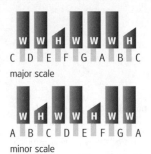

C D E F G A B C
major scale

A B C D E F G A
minor scale

The major and minor scales
have different outlines.

whole step

half step

More scales

Each time you start the circle on page 59 on another note, you will get a different order of whole and half steps: You will hear a different scale each time, each with a different character due to the changing order of whole and half steps! This chapter deals with the two most popular scales: major and minor. Other scales are covered in Chapter 14.

MAJOR SCALES

A major scale can start on C or any other note. All you have to do is make sure that the order of the steps remains the same as in C-major: W, W, H, W, W, W, H. This sounds harder than it is.

The order of the steps

Chapter 4 demonstrated that you can begin 'Twinkle, Twinkle' on C, but also on F or D. In order to make it *sound* like 'Twinkle, Twinkle,' one note had to be lowered when you played it in F. When played in D, one note had to be raised. In other words: You raised or lowered notes to maintain the desired tonal distances. With scales, it's just the same.

From F to F

If you play the white keys from F to F, for example, the order of whole and half steps is W, W, W, H, W, W, H. No keyboard at hand? Then check the circle on page 59. This order does not correspond with the order of the major scale: The first half step has moved from the third to the fourth position. You can hear the difference, and you can clearly see the difference below.

major scale

no major scale

The steps from C to C and from F to F, played on the white keys only; the difference is obvious. From F to F is not a major scale: The order of Ws and Hs is different.

F-major in columns

To play a major scale starting on F, all you have to do is change the order of whole and half steps. You do so, in this case, by lowering the B. This turns it into B♭. As a result, you get the 'major' order of whole and half steps, starting on F: the F-major scale!

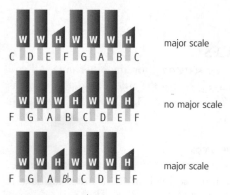

major scale

no major scale

major scale

Turning a B into a B♭ corrects the order of the steps in this scale.

F-major on the staff   Tipcode MOP-032

Moving over to the keyboard, here's the difference between playing the white notes from F to F (no major scale) and lowering the B to a B♭: Then, you hear a major scale.

G-major

In the example on the next page, a flat was added. If you start a scale at other notes, you may need more flats, or one or more sharps to turn it into a major scale. If, for example, you go from G to the next higher G on the white keys, you will find that the order of the last two steps differs from that of the major scale: W, H instead of H, W.

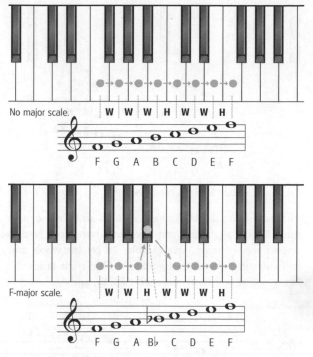

No major scale.

W W W H W W H

F G A B C D E F

F-major scale.

W W H W W W H

F G A Bb C D E F

Lowering the B to a Bb turns this sequence into a F-major scale.

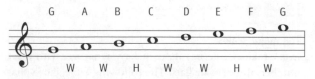

G A B C D E F G

W W H W W H W

The natural notes from G. The order of the last two steps does not correspond with the major scale.

An F with a sharp

In this example, things go wrong from E to F. This is a half step, but it should be a whole step to make this a major scale. The solution is to raise, or *sharpen*, the F. Then the *last* step will automatically change from whole to half, which is exactly what you need to create the scale of G-major.

After the clef

If a piece is written in G-major, you won't find a sharp in front of every F. Instead, there's a single sharp at the clef.

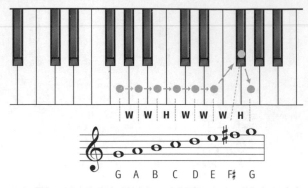

The scale of G-major: The F has been raised.

That one sharp, the key signature, turns all Fs in the piece into F♯s. Key signatures can have anywhere from zero to seven flats or sharps. An example: To get the whole and half steps in the scale of E♭-major in the right order, the *key signature* will show three flats: B♭, E♭, and A♭.

The scale of E♭-major, with three flats.

The major scales

Every major scale has its own key signature, with a set number of sharps or flats. The following table shows that number for each key signature, and it tells you which notes are raised or lowered. Page 128 shows the major scales on a staff.

Always the same

As you may remember from pages 32–33 , the sharps and flats 'appear in a fixed order': The sharps and flats in a key signature always refer to the same notes. If there's just one sharp, it raises every F to an F♯. If the key signature shows two sharps, every C is raised as well – and so on.

The number tells it all

Likewise, one flat turns every B into a B♭; the second flat lowers every E too, the third also lowers every A, and so

MAJOR SCALES

key signature	tonic	sharps and flats	
C-major	C	0	
G-major	G	**1** ♯	F♯
D-major	D	**2** ♯♯	F♯, C♯
A-major	A	**3** ♯♯ ♯	F♯, C♯, G♯
E-major	E	**4** ♯♯ ♯♯	F♯, C♯, G♯, D♯
B-major	B	**5** ♯♯ ♯♯ ♯	F♯, C♯, G♯, D♯, A♯
F♯-major	F♯	**6** ♯♯ ♯♯ ♯♯	F♯, C♯, G♯, D♯, A♯, E♯
G♭-major	G♭	**6** ♭♭ ♭♭ ♭♭	B♭, E♭, A♭, D♭, G♭, C♭
D♭-major	D♭	**5** ♭♭ ♭♭ ♭	B♭, E♭, A♭, D♭, G♭
A♭-major	A♭	**4** ♭♭ ♭♭	B♭, E♭, A♭, D♭
E♭-major	E♭	**3** ♭♭ ♭	B♭, E♭, A♭
B♭-major	B♭	**2** ♭♭	B♭, E♭
F-major	F	**1** ♭	B♭

Major scales. The scales of F♯-major and G♭-major sound the same; they are enharmonic equivalent (see page 34).

on. The number of sharps or flats in the key signature tells you right away which notes to raise or lower.

Not so difficult

A piece with four or five sharps or flats looks more complicated than it is; with a bit of practice and talent, you'll find that you play the right notes almost automatically. And once you've grabbed the system underlying the order of the sharps and flats, things become even easier. This system is covered in the next chapter.

One tone

If the order of the whole and half steps in all those major scales is always the same, then why isn't everything written in C-major? Wouldn't it be easier without all those sharps and flats? Yes, it would. But it would also make things pretty monotonous (which literally means 'one tone').

A little different

Besides, a piece in F-major not only sounds higher or lower than the same piece in C-major, it also sounds a little *different*. That is because each key, like each color, has a certain character. That's why composers often deliberately choose a certain scale for a certain piece.

MINOR SCALES

The section above applies to minor scales as well. The only difference is that minor scales have a different order of whole and half steps.

From A to A: A-minor
Tipcode MOP-033

If you play all the natural notes from one A to the next, the whole steps and half steps will be in the following order: W, H, W, W, H, W, W. This is the scale of A-minor.

The scale of A-minor.

C-minor

If you want to play a minor scale starting on C (C-minor), you will have to lower three notes: B, E, and A.

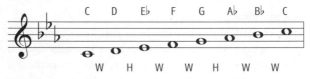

C-minor has three flats (B♭, E♭, and A♭).

Three lowered notes

A minor scale sounds so different from a major scale because three notes are lowered: the third, the sixth, and the seventh. This is often shown as 1-2-♭3-4-5-♭6-♭7. In C, those lowered notes would be, as noted above, the E (3), the A (6), and the B (7).

The lowered third
Tipcode MOP-034

The different characters of minor and major stem mainly from the lowered third note. To hear the effect, play the major chord C–E–G followed by the minor chord C–E♭–G. The first chord sounds bright and clear; the second sounds quite dark, sad, or melancholic.

MINOR SCALES

key signature	tonic	sharps and flats	
A-minor	A	0	
E-minor	E	**1** ♯	F♯
B-minor	B	**2** ♯♯	F♯, C♯
F♯-minor	F♯	**3** ♯♯ ♯	F♯, C♯, G♯
C♯-minor	C♯	**4** ♯♯ ♯♯	F♯, C♯, G♯, D♯
G♯-minor	G♯	**5** ♯♯ ♯♯ ♯	F♯, C♯, G♯, D♯, A♯
D♯-minor	D♯	**6** ♯♯ ♯♯ ♯♯	F♯, C♯, G♯, D♯, A♯, E♯
E♭-minor	E♭	**6** ♭♭ ♭♭ ♭♭	B♭, E♭, A♭, D♭, G♭, C♭
B♭-minor	B♭	**5** ♭♭ ♭♭ ♭	B♭, E♭, A♭, D♭, G♭,
F-minor	F	**4** ♭♭ ♭♭	B♭, E♭, A♭, D♭
C-minor	C	**3** ♭♭ ♭	B♭, E♭, A♭
G-minor	G	**2** ♭♭	B♭, E♭
D-minor	D	**1** ♭	B♭

Minor scales. The scales of D♯-minor and E♭-minor sound the same; they are enharmonic equivalent (see page 34).

The same order

As you can see above, the sharps and flats appear in the same order as they do in major scales!

Scale wheel

The scale wheel on page 127 is a handy device to find the notes of the major and minor scales. It also clearly demonstrates that the order of whole and half steps is the same in any major scale – and the same goes for minor scales, of course.

OTHER NOTES

Most pieces are based on the notes of one particular scale – but that doesn't mean that all notes in a piece belong to that scale. You may very well come across accidental sharps or flats in a piece in C major or A minor, though both key signatures are without sharps or flats.

Modulation

In some pieces, the music changes key. This is known as *modulation*. A piece that modulates starts in one key, goes to one or more other keys in the middle, and then often returns to the first key. If a piece modulates, the key signature doesn't necessarily change – any extra sharps, flats, or natural signs are written as accidentals. Sometimes, however, you'll see a new key signature written on the staff, after a section line.

11. THE CIRCLE OF FIFTHS

The fixed order of the sharps and flats is not coincidental. There's a system behind it. The circle of fifths, which is based on that system, shows you at a glance how many sharps or flats there are in a given scale.

In the previous chapter, you saw that C-major has no sharps or flats. G-major has one sharp (F♯). D-major has two (F♯, C♯), A-major has three (F♯, C♯, G♯) – and so on.

A fifth higher

If you go from the root of the major scale without sharps (C) to the root of the major scale with one sharp (G), you'll count five white notes. This tonal distance or *interval* is known as a *fifth*: G is a fifth higher than C.

Another fifth up

If you move from G to the root of the scale with two sharps (D), you go up another fifth. And from D to A (three sharps) is a fifth too. In other words, a sharp is added for every major scale that starts a fifth higher.

C D E F **G** A B C
G A B C **D** E F♯ G
D E F♯ G **A** B C♯ D

A sharp is added every time you start the next scale five notes higher.

The raised seventh

There's yet another pattern. Every time you move a fifth up for the next major scale, the added sharp raises the *seventh step* or *degree* of that scale. The F♯ is the seventh step of the scale of G. C♯ is the seventh note of the scale of D – and so on.

Hearing it

You can hear this too. First play the white notes from C to the next higher C. Now play the white notes from G to G: The seventh step (F) is too low. Raise it to F♯ and you're playing a major scale again.

Flats: a fifth lower

Scales with one or more flats have similar patterns. To find the next scale, you start a fifth lower: C-major has no flats. F-major (a fifth lower) has one flat. B♭-major (again a fifth lower) has two flats – and so on.

C D E **F** G A B C

F G A **B♭** C D E **F**

B♭ C D **E♭** F G A **B♭**

A flat is added every time you start a scale a fifth lower.

The lowered fourth note

The 'new' flat of the next scale always lowers the *fourth note* of that scale: B♭ is the fourth note of the scale of F; E♭ is the fourth note of the scale of B♭ – and so on.

CIRCLE OF FIFTHS

The *circle of fifths* is a very handy tool that shows all major scales. If you start at C and go round clockwise, you will see that a sharp is added in every succeeding scale. Go around counterclockwise, and a flat is added each time.

Like a clock

Just like a clock, the circle of fifths is divided into twelve. There are five minutes between the numbers on the face of a clock. Similarly, there's always a distance of five steps (a fifth) from one scale to the other. Go one fifth clockwise, from the top, and a sharp is added. Go one fifth counterclockwise, and a flat is added.

How many sharps or flats

Memory joggers can help you remember the number of flats and sharps for each major scale.

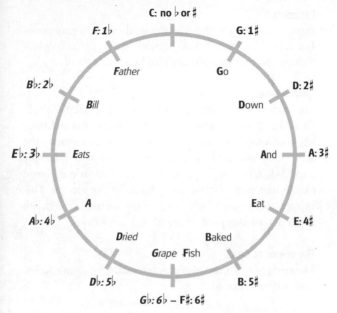

The circle of fifths with all the major scales.

Major scales with sharps

The scale of G-major has one sharp, D-major has two, and so on: **Go** (1) **Down** (2) **And** (3) **Eat** (4) **Baked** (5) **Fish** (F♯: 6 sharps).

Major scales with flats

F-major has one flat, B♭ has two, E♭ has three, and so on: **Father** (1) **Bill** (2) **Eats** (3) **A** (4) **Dried** (5) **Grape** (G♭: 6 flats).

Father Charles

Another memory aid helps you with the order of the sharps and flats. The sharps show up in the following order: **Father Charles Goes Down And Ends Battle** (F♯, C♯, G♯, D♯, A♯, E♯, B♯.

In other words, one sharp turns each F into an F♯; the second sharp tells you to play a C♯ for every C – and so on.

Battle Ends

The same line in reverse order tells you which notes to lower for any number of flats: **Battle Ends And Down Goes Charles' Father** (B♭, E♭, A♭, D♭, G♭, C♭, F♭).

Fat cows

Instead of having Father Charles go down, you may prefer Fat Cows Go Dancing At Emily's Barn, for example – though this one doesn't work backwards.

Enharmonics

The bottom of the circle of fifths shows G♭-major with six flats and F♯-major with six sharps. These scales and their key signatures look different, but they sound exactly the same: G♭-major and F♯-major are *enharmonic scales* (see page 34). Likewise, a piece in seven flats would sound exactly the same as the same piece in five sharps. This explains why you'll only very rarely see signatures with seven flats or sharps: You can always do with less.

The minor scales

The circle of fifths can also accommodate the minor scales, as shown on page 84.

12. INTERVALS

Previous chapters introduced the octave and the fifth as names for 'musical distances' from one note to another. The technical term for these distances is intervals. Knowledge of intervals isn't required to play music – but it is essential if you want to understand music.

Like scales, *intervals* have their own character. Try playing a C and a G together, followed by a C and a Db. The first combination sounds fine, the second one sounds pretty mean. The effect of this variety of characters or colors is added color and expressiveness, no matter what the style of music.

Second, third, fourth, fifth

G is the fifth step (the fifth note) in the scale of C-major. The name of this interval (C–G) is a fifth. The names of most intervals are based on the steps or degrees in a major scale. From C to D is a second, from C to E a third, and so on.

In every scale

It's just the same in other scales: from F to G is a second; from F to A is a third – and so on. To keep things simple, the scale of C-major is used is most examples in this chapter.

Unison and octave

There is of course no 'musical distance' between two notes of the same pitch, yet there's a name for this interval too: *unison*, which literally means 'one sound.' The *octave* is the eighth step (*e.g.*, from C to the next higher C, or from A to the next A: eight white notes). This term comes from the Latin word *octo*, meaning eight.

On the staff
Tipcode MOP-035

On a staff, the eight basic intervals of the C-major scale look like this:

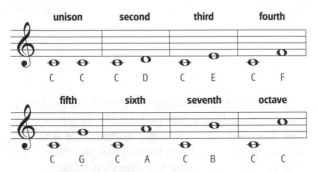

Intervals between C and the notes of C-major.

PERFECT AND MAJOR

The eight basic intervals are divided into *perfect intervals* and *major intervals*.

Perfect intervals
Tipcode MOP-036

Four intervals are called *perfect* because they have an almost perfect, pure sound: the unison (C–C), the fourth (C–F), the fifth (C–G), and the octave (C–C). When you play each pair of notes, you'll find that the seem to fuse together – especially the octave, which tends to sound like one note only.

Major intervals
Tipcode MOP-037

The other four intervals are known as *major intervals*; the second (C–D), the third (C–E), the sixth (C–A), and the seventh (C–B). If you play them, you'll hear that they sound noticeably different than the perfect intervals. Especially the second and the seventh: They're much less 'perfect' than the perfect intervals. The third and the sixth are somewhere in between.

MINOR, DIMINISHED, AUGMENTED

The distance from C to G is a fifth. From C to A is a sixth.

But you can also go from C to G♯, for example. Here's how you name these 'in-between' intervals.

Perfect, diminished, and augmented
If you reduce a perfect interval by a half step (C–G →C–G♭) it becomes *diminished*.
If you enlarge a perfect interval by a half step (C–G →C–G♯), it becomes *augmented*.

dimished ◄──── *reduce* ──── **perfect** ──── *enlarge* ────► **augmented**

Major, minor, and augmented
If you reduce a major interval by a half step (C–A →C–A♭) it becomes *minor*.
If you enlarge a major interval by a half step (C–A →C–A♯) it becomes *augmented*.

minor ◄──── *reduce* ──── **major** ──── *enlarge* ────► **augmented**

Minor reduced once more
A minor interval can be made smaller once more; it then becomes a diminished interval.

FIFTEEN INTERVALS
Below are the fifteen most common intervals. The perfect and major intervals are listed to the left of the keyboard; the minor and diminished intervals to the right, and the augmented intervals are on the far right. Other intervals, such as the augmented unison (C–C♯), are quite rare.

Same sound, different name
Just as there are enharmonic notes (see page 37), there are *enharmonic intervals* too: intervals that sound the same, but have different names. For example, C–G♯ is an augmented fifth and C–A♭ is a minor sixth – but both span eight half steps, and you play them on the same keys.

Larger intervals
All the intervals introduced so far have been within the space of one octave. Bigger intervals work in exactly the same way – you just keep counting. From C to the D of the next octave is a *major ninth*, or to the E of the next octave

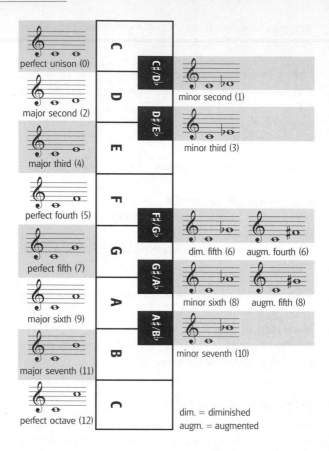

Fifteen intervals starting on the root C. The number of half steps of each interval is given in parentheses.

is a *major tenth*. Such intervals are frequently used to indicate chords, as you'll see in chapter 18.

Major up, minor down   Tipcode MOP-038

If you go from C to a higher sounding E, it's a *major* third. If you go from C to the E below, you're playing a *minor* sixth. The same goes for every other pair of notes that form a major interval one way: They form a minor interval when inverted – *i.e.*, when the lower note and the higher one switch positions. Major scales consist of perfect and major intervals when you go upward from the root. But going down (C to the B below, C to the A below, and so on) you'll find perfect and minor intervals only.

Know the root

To correctly name an interval in the context of a piece of music, you need to know the root note of the piece. If a song in C starts on a G, and the second note is a C, you go four steps down. You're not playing a fourth, however, but a (downward) fifth: After all, G is the fifth step of the key of C.

Not just the white notes

Another potential mistake: On a piano keyboard, F–B may look like a perfect fourth, as it spans four white notes, just like C–F. But F–B is not a perfect fourth: It's an augmented fourth. If you want to name an interval, you need to take the major scale of the root note into account. In F-major, the fourth step is B♭, so F–B♭ is a perfect fourth; F–B is an augmented fourth.

Half steps

If you're not sure, you can always count the number of half steps in an interval. A perfect fifth, for example, always consists of seven half steps. If you count eight half steps, you're looking at an augmented fifth or a minor sixth. The number of half steps of each interval are given in parentheses in the diagram on the opposite page.

Tritone   Tipcode MOP-039

The enharmonic augmented fourth (C–F♯) and diminished fifth (C–G♭) are also known as *tritone*: an interval spanning three whole steps (from C to D, D to E, and E to F♯).

Well-known tunes

The easiest way to learn to recognize intervals by ear is by using the first notes of well-known songs. Some examples are listed on page 79.

CONSONANT AND DISSONANT

Intervals can also be classified as either *dissonant* or *consonant*. Dissonant literally means 'not sounding (well) together'. The notes in a dissonant interval seem to *dis*agree. They're not out of tune with each other, and their combined sound is not really nasty or less attractive, but it definitely feels as if there is tension between them.

The name's obvious

Tipcode MOP-040

The dissonant intervals are the minor and major seconds, the enharmonic augmented fourth and diminished fifth, and the minor and major sevenths. There's no need to learn them by heart. Just play them, and you'll hear why they're called dissonant.

Consonant

Consonant is the opposite of dissonant. The notes in a consonant interval seem to blend into each other. They offer the release that the tension in dissonant intervals seems to ask for.

(Im)perfect consonant

Tipcode MOP-041

The consonant intervals can be subdivided once more, into *perfect* and *imperfect consonant* intervals. The imperfect ones just sound a bit less 'perfect' or pure. Again, listening to these intervals clearly demonstrates their names.
- Perfect consonant intervals are the perfect unison, fourth, fifth, and the octave.
- Imperfect consonant intervals are the major and minor thirds, and the major and minor sixths.

Release

Tipcode MOP-042

In many styles of music there's a lot of flux and play between the tension of dissonant intervals and the *release* offered by the consonant ones. If you play the notes C–F♯ together, followed by C–G, you'll hear what's happening: tension and release.

INTERVAL RECOGNITION

It can be useful to be able to recognize intervals by ear, and to be able to 'hear' them in your head: This will help you to sing or imagine chords or melodies on paper without an instrument, and it makes it a lot easier to write music and to transcribe songs.

Ear training

One way to learn how to recognize intervals is by figuring out melodies on an instrument without printed music. Or you can have someone play intervals for you and see if you can recognize them. Alternatively, there are computer programs and pre-recorded cassettes that offer this kind of *ear training* too.

Well-known tunes

The easiest way to remember the sound of an interval is simply to find a tune that begins with that interval. Here are some examples.

Minor second	Symphony no. 40 (W.A. Mozart)
Major second	Frère Jacques, Frère Jacques
Minor third	Greensleeves: 'Alas, My Love'
Major third	Oh, When The Saints
Perfect fourth	Amazing Grace
Augmented fourth	Maria (Westside story)
Perfect fifth	Twinkle, Twinkle, Little Star; It Ain't Necessarily So
Major sixth	My Bonnie Lies Over The Ocean
Minor seventh	Somewhere: 'There's A Place For Us'
Octave	Somewhere Over The Rainbow

With these tunes in mind it is easy to memorize these intervals.
Please note, however, the comments about naming intervals on page 77 (Know the root).

13. MORE ABOUT MAJOR AND MINOR

There's more to major and minor than what you've read up to now. This chapter covers variations on the minor scale, relative keys, and recognizing key signatures. Apart from enhancing your understanding of music, this information will be useful if you want to transcribe or write music.

Most Western music is written either in major or minor. They are the two most important *modes*. Both modes can be indicated in several ways.

Major

If a piece is just said to be 'in G,' it is in G-major. And a D-chord is a D-major chord. To prevent confusion, however, the word *major* or its abbreviation *maj.* may be written after the letter. In classical music you may also come across the German word for major, *dur*.

Minor

A minor key or chord is usually specified by the word *minor*, or the abbreviations *min* or *m* after the letter: Dm is D-minor. Other ways to indicate the minor mode are a minus sign (D–), a lower-case letter (d) or the German word for minor, *moll*.

Major	Minor
upper case (C)	lower case (c)
maj.	min, m, –
dur (German)	moll (German)

A variety of indications for the two most important modes.

THE LEADING NOTE

In the major mode, there is a half step between the seventh and eighth notes (*e.g.*, B–C). As a result, the seventh note tends to 'lead' the music toward the root: It is called the *leading note*. The minor mode has a lowered seventh, which places a whole step between the seventh and eighth notes (*e.g.*, B♭–C). Due to this whole step, the minor mode does not have a leading note.

Subtonic

The leading note is also known as the *subtonic*: the note that is literally 'right' under (sub) the tonic, or root.

Leading note   Tipcode MOP-043

In C-major, B (the seventh step) is the leading note. In the following example you can hear how B leads to C.

The B leads to the C.   leading note

Rock and pop

The leading note is not equally important in all styles of music. Thousands of rock songs in a major key actually have a flattened seventh, and therefore no leading note. This altered major scale with a flattened seventh is also known as the *Mixolydian* mode (see page 88).

Jazz

Jazz musicians uses a wide variety of scales, including standard and altered major and minor. The minor scale is sometimes altered to create a leading note.

Classical music

Classical composers often alter the minor scale to create a leading note, as it is so important in classical music. Two of these alterations are *melodic minor* and *harmonic minor*.

MELODIC AND HARMONIC MINOR

Below are two tunes. The first one, in D-minor, lacks a leading note. In the second one, the C is raised to C♯ to create a leading note. If you play it, you'll hear it clearly leads the melody toward the final D.

Tipcode MOP-044

D-minor without a leading note.

The same tune, now with a leading note.

Up or down

The alteration of a minor scale to create a raised seventh in a melody is known as *melodic minor*. Because the leading note always wants to rise to the root, it's not suitable for descending melodies. That's why melodic minor is considered a 'two-way' scale: It has a raised seventh when it goes up, and it doesn't when it goes down.

Raise the sixth step too

Tipcode MOP-045

In the rising version of melodic minor, the sixth step is raised too. Why? Raising the seventh step to form a leading note creates a gap of three half steps between the sixth and seventh steps. (In C, this would be from A♭ to the raised B.) This interval sounds awkward in a melody. Raising the sixth reduces the gap to a whole step (A–B).

One difference

With that, the only difference between a major scale and the melodic minor scale with the same root is the lowered third, since the other two notes that turned major to minor have been raised to their original pitches: C melodic minor is C, D, E♭, F, G, A, B, C.

Harmonic minor

Harmonic minor is another alteration of the minor scale. It has a raised seventh; the third and sixth remain lowered, with the large gap between the sixth and seventh step (*e.g.*, C, D, E♯, F, G, A♭, B, C).

Accidentals

The rising melodic minor scale and the harmonic minor

scale are only alterations of the natural minor scale, so you won't find a piece 'in G harmonic minor,' for example. If a piece in G minor makes use of G melodic minor and G harmonic minor, these alterations are scored with accidentals. The example below is in D-minor, which has one flat in the key signature. The natural signs that raise the B♭ to a B and the C to a C♯ come from the melodic minor scale.

Tune in D minor using the rising melodic minor scale, with a raised sixth (B) and seventh (C♯) step.

RELATIVE MAJOR AND MINOR

If you want to transcribe a song from a CD, for example, you need to know which key it is in. In order to do so, you need to know a bit more about scales.

Two scales

In Chapter 10 all major and minor scales are listed. If you look at the tables on pages 65 and 67, you'll see that there are two scales without flats and sharps (C-major on the first line of the table on page 65; A-minor on the first line of the table on page 67). There are also two scales with one sharp, two scales with three, and so on.

Relative scales

These pairs of scales, using the same notes and the same key signature, are *relative scales* or *relative keys*. For example, A-minor (A, B, C, D, E, F, G, A) is the *relative minor* of C-major (C, D, E, F, G, A, B, C): The notes, though in a different order, are the same, and the key signature is the same, but the scales have a different root.

Two sharps, two flats

Likewise, D-major (two sharps) is the *relative major* of B-minor (again, two sharps.); G-minor (two flats) is the relative minor of B♭-major (again, two flats).

Relative minor

Finding the relative minor of a given major scale is simply

a matter of counting. The relative minor is always indicated by the sixth step of the major scale. Two examples:

- D-minor is the relative minor of F-major; D is the sixth step of F-major (F, G, A, Bb, C, **D**, E, F).
- E-minor is the relative minor of G-major; E is the sixth step of G-major (G, A, B, C, D, **E**, F♯, G).

Relative major

You will find the *relative major* of a minor key by looking at the third step of the minor scale. Two examples:

- C-major is the relative major of A-minor (A, B, **C**, D, E, F, G, A).
- The relative major of C-minor (C, D, **E**b, F, G, Ab, Bb, C) is Eb-major.

Once again: the circle of fifths

When fitting the minor keys into the circle of fifths, they are automatically paired with their relative major keys.

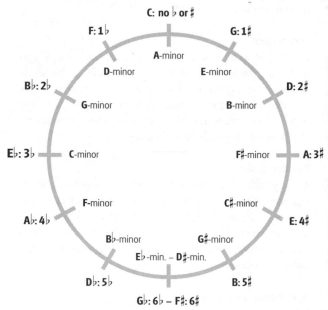

The circle of fifths showing relative major keys (outer circle) and minor keys (inner circle).

Parallel keys

Parallel keys are sometimes confused with relative keys. The difference: Relative keys have the same key signature and a different root. Parallel keys have the same root and a different key signature, such as C major (no sharps, no flats) and C-minor (three flats).

FIGURING OUT KEYS

It's often useful to be able to figure out what key a piece is in, whether you're playing from sheet music, transcribing a song from a recording, or playing a solo over a CD.

First: the root   Tipcode MOP-046

To figure out the key, you need to know the root note of a piece. This is nearly always the note a melody ends on. The moment you feel the song is over, chances are, nine out of ten, that you're listening to the root. In the following two melodies it is fairly easy to sense what the root is. Just play them and stop right before the last note – you'll probably be able to sing it before you play it: It's the root or the home note.

If you play these melodies, you can 'hear' the last note before you've played it.

F-major or D-minor?

Both melodies above have a single flat in the key signature. This tells you they're either in F-major or its relative D-minor. Which one is it? The root note at the end usually provides the correct answer. The first tune ends on an F, so it's in F-major; the second one ends on D, and it's in D-minor.

The D-minor scale.

Trick

If you're looking at a key signature and you don't know the key a certain number of flats or sharps refers to (and you don't have a circle of fifths at hand to tell you), here's what you can do.

Pointing sharps

If it's a key signature with sharps, then look at the final sharp, and go a half step up. This note is the root note if the piece is in a major key. If not, it's in its relative minor key.

The second-to-last flat

In flat key signatures, it's even easier. The second-to-last flat tells you the possible major key. If it's in minor, it's the relative minor of that key.

The last sharp (D♯) points to the E. Therefore the key is E-major, or its relative, C♯-minor.

The second-to-last flat refers to the D♭, so this piece is in D♭-major, or its relative, B♭-minor.

By ear

Figuring out the key of a piece of music by ear, from CD for example, is a bit harder.

- First figure out the root by listening to the final note of the piece, or by listening to other places where the melody seems to come to a rest.
- Sing the root when you have found it, and use an instrument to find out which note it is.
- Now try out both the major and minor scales that begin with that note (they're all written out on pages 128 and 129). In most cases, you'll be able to hear which of the two scales best matches the music. This will usually be the key.

Sounds easier

The above sounds easier than it really is, especially if you're just starting out. A tip: First try this with very basic, familiar melodies such as children's songs.

14. OTHER SCALES

All major and minor scales are made up of five whole and two half steps. By mixing the order of whole and half steps, you can create another five scales. In addition, there are scales that use different combinations of intervals. This chapter takes you from medieval church music to modal jazz, and from China to the blues.

In Chapter 10, the C-major and A-minor scales were illustrated using a circle made up of half steps and whole steps.

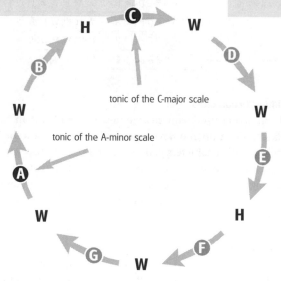

tonic of the C-major scale

tonic of the A-minor scale

Playing clockwise from C produces C-major.
If you start on A, you get A-minor.

Different orders

Each time you play this circle from another note, you'll play a different scale; their different characters are the result of a different order of whole and half steps, as discussed in Chapter 10.

Traditional modes

The resulting seven scales are usually referred to as the *traditional modes* or *church modes*, as they were the basis of Roman Catholic church music in the Middle Ages. The Ionian mode is similar to the modern major scale; the *Aeolian mode* is similar to the minor scale. These two scales were only added much later, in the sixteenth century.

White notes

You can play these scales using white notes only, as shown below:

Mode	A.k.a.	Played on white notes	Whole and half steps
Dorian	D-mode	D E F G A B C D	W, H, W, W, W, H, W
Phrygian	E-mode	E F G A B C D E	H, W, W, W, H, W, W
Lydian	F-mode	F G A B C D E F	W, W, W, H, W, W, H
Mixolydian	G-mode	G A B C D E F G	W, W, H, W, W, H, W
Aeolian	A-mode	A B C D E F G A	W, H, W, W, H, W, W
Locrian	B-mode	B C D E F G A B	H, W, W, H, W, W, W
Ionian	C-mode	C D E F G A B C	W, W, H, W, W, W, H

Different characters

If you play around with these modes a bit, rather than just playing them up and down the scale, you will get to hear their specific characters. Some examples? The Mixolydian mode is often heard in pop songs and boogie-woogie. Playing around in the Phrygian mode may make you think of Spanish music, and the Locrian mode tends to sounds jazzy.

Two extremes

To hear how different they sound, you can also play the traditional scales starting on the same root – which is just a matter of copying the whole and half steps. The Lydian and Locrian modes are written out below, both starting on C:

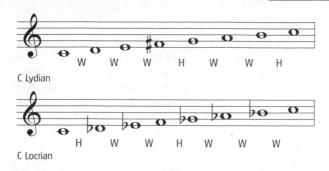

C Lydian

C Locrian

Modal music

The term *modal music* is sometimes used for music in which the character of the traditional modes is clearly identifiable. Usually there's not much harmonic activity in this type of music. In other words, you won't hear too many chord changes. In classical music, the church modes weren't used much after around 1600 until the late nineteenth century, when certain composers started using them again.

Modal jazz

There's also non-classical modal music. In the late 1950s jazz trumpeter Miles Davis stopped relying on the chord changes that were essential in bebop, the style of jazz that was developed in the 1940s. Davis then started writing what became known as *modal jazz*. His album 'Kind of Blue' (1959) clearly demonstrates what that is like.

Diatonic scales

The traditional modes are also known as *diatonic modes*. All seven consist of five whole steps and two half steps. Diatonic scales actually have two (*dia* = two) tonics or roots. For C Ionic (C-major) the first is C; the second is G. If you take look at a keyboard, you can easily see that this scale consists of two identical halves: C, D, E, F and G, A, B, C. Both halves consist of three whole steps and one half step in the same order. These halves are called *tetrachords*. The second tonic is the tonic of the second tetrachord.

NON-DIATONIC SCALES Tipcode MOP-047

The following scales are all quite different from the diatonic ones. For one thing, they have different numbers of whole and half steps.

Chromatic

The *chromatic* scale uses all twelve notes in the octave: It's built up entirely of half steps. This scale is great for practicing, just going up and down, playing every single note on your instrument. A variation: Start on another note each time. You'll find this scale – and many ways to fool around with it – in lots of exercise books.

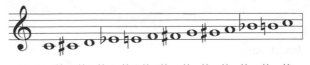

H H H   H H H H   H H H H   H

The chromatic scale.

Hexatonic

The *hexatonic* scale or *whole-tone scale* consists of whole steps only, which results in a six-note scale (not including high C). *Hexa* means six.

W   W   W   W   W   W

Hexatonic scale

Octatonic

Octatonic scales (*octa* means eight, as in octave) have alternating half and whole steps. They're often used in jazz and twentieth-century classical music. There are two versions: one starting with a whole step, the other with a half step.

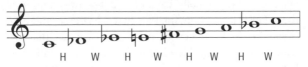

H   W   H   W   H   W   H   W

An octatonic scale, starting with a half step.

Pentatonic scales

Pentatonic scales (*penta* = five) are used in many different styles: You can hear them in country, pop, and folk, but they can have a definite Chinese flavor as well. Want to hear that flavor? Try playing two-note combinations of black keys, keeping one black key between each pair (*e.g.*, F#–A#, G#–C#, A#–D#).

W   W   HHH   W   HHH

A pentatonic scale.

Blues scales

There are several different blues scales. Pictured below is a classic one.

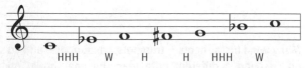

HHH   W   H   H   HHH   W

A classic blues scale.

The gypsy scale

The so-called gypsy scale is also easy to recognize. Just like the blues scale, it has two intervals of three half steps (E♭–F♯ and A♭–B).

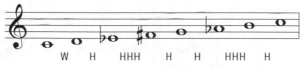

W   H   HHH   H   H   HHH   H

The gypsy scale.

15. TRANSPOSITION

Many wind instruments – trumpets, saxophones, and so on – sound a different note than the one shown on paper: They are transposing instruments. If you want to write music for transposing instruments, you need to transpose it. Knowing how to do this also allows you to change the key of a song if it needs to be played higher or lower.

When tenor sax players see a C5 on paper (third space, treble clef) they close the key under their left middle finger – they *finger* a C. When they blow, though, the note you hear is a B♭, a whole step lower.

B♭ instruments
In other words: On a tenor saxophone, a fingered C results in a *B♭ concert pitch* or a *sounding B♭*. Hence, the tenor saxophone is a B♭ instrument. Soprano saxophones are in B♭ as well, and so are most trumpets and clarinets.

E♭ instruments
E♭ instruments, such as alto and baritone saxophones, produce an E♭ when a C is read and fingered.

The same fingering   Tipcode MOP-048
This may sound a little complicated, but it has one great advantage. No matter which sax you're playing, you always use the same fingerings. A C5 on paper always tells you to close the key under your left middle finger. The note you'll hear is the note the composer wanted to hear: The saxophone 'transposes' the written note to the desired pitch.

On paper: Concert pitches:

soprano alto tenor baritone

The note C5 on paper, the corresponding fingering C for all saxes, and the resulting concert pitches.

Lower sound, higher note

As you can see, the soprano saxophone sounds a whole step lower than the written note: C5 on paper produces a Bb4. This means that composers write music for the soprano sax a whole step higher then the notes they wants to hear. The tenor saxophone sounds a ninth lower than the written note: C5 produces Bb3, so the composer writes every note a ninth higher than he or she wants to hear it.

Other instruments and tunings

There are many transposing wind instruments. Trumpets and various other brass instruments are available in different tunings (e.g., Bb, Eb, D, C). Clarinets are produced in a wide variety of voices and tunings, including the popular A- and Bb-clarinets. French horns come in Bb and F, alto flutes are in G, and there are alto and bass recorders in F.

An octave

For some instruments the music is written either an octave higher or lower than it sounds, which avoids having to use many ledger lines. Music for guitar and bass, for example, is written an octave higher than it sounds, while music for the high-pitched piccolo is written an octave lower. This also helps to avoid ledger lines. Because a fingered C produces a C, these instruments are not classified as transposing instruments.

TRANSPOSING

If you write music for transposing instruments, you have to be able to transpose. You also have to transpose if you want to play a piece in another key. Why would you want to do that? If in the current key some notes are too high or too low for the singer, for example, or to make certain chords easier to finger.

Sounds harder than it is

Transposing sounds harder than it is. Without knowing it, you've already transposed 'Twinkle, Twinkle' from C to F and also to D in Chapter 4. Transposing music also demonstrates how efficient the system of sharps and flats actually is.

In a nutshell

To transpose a piece of music, the first thing to do is change the key signature to the new key. Then, you move all the notes to their new positions on the staff – and that's all!

How to do it

Say you have a part in C-major, and you want to transpose it to E♭-major. This makes it sound a minor third higher (from C to E♭ is a minor third).

- E♭-minor has three flats, as you can see in the circle of fifths.
- Jot down these three flats (B♭, E♭, A♭) next to the clef, in their proper positions (see page 33).
- E♭ is a minor third higher than C. A third involves three steps, so you move all notes three steps up, including their original position.
- That's all.

'Twinkle, Twinkle' transposed from C to E♭. The three flats are at the clef. The original notes are in gray; the new notes in black.

Naturals, sharps, and flats

So really, transposing is no more than figuring out the sharps and flats of the new key, and moving the notes up or down on the staff. The desired number of sharps or flats can easily be found in the circle of fifths. The name of the interval tells you how far you have to move the notes up or down: two positions if it's a second; three if it's a third, and so on.

Minor, major

Transposing from C to E♭, 'Twinkle, Twinkle' went up a minor third. If you want to transpose the same tune from C to E (now a major third), the notes will be moved to the same positions as in the above example, only the key signature will have four sharps: E-major has four sharps.

From E♭ to B

Transposing a piece from E♭ to B is just as easy as from C to E♭, for example:
- B-major has five sharps. Write them down next to the clef.
- The interval E♭–B is an augmented fifth (E♭, F, G, A, B).
- If the notes are to be transposed a fifth higher, move them up five steps, including the original and the final position. This equals two lines on the staff.

Twin - kle,   twin - kle   lit - tle   star

'Twinkle, Twinkle' transposed from E♭ to B. The original notes are in gray, the new notes in black. The three flats of E♭-major have been replaced by the five sharps of B-major.

Transposing accidentals

If a note has an accidental, things get a little bit more complicated: A sharp or flat sign may need to be turned into a natural sign, or vice versa. In the following example, a melody is transposed from B♭-major to G-major. The new key signature is put in place, and the notes are moved three places down the stave. In the original, the natural sign before the E raised the fourth step of B♭-major (E♭). Therefore, the fourth step in G-major (C) has to be raised too, so the C gets a sharp.

A tune transposed from B♭-major to G-major. The natural sign becomes a sharp.

95

16. TIME, METER, AND RHYTHM

A chapter on strong beats and weak beats, odd time signatures, single and compound meters, swing, and the clave.

In a piece in $\frac{4}{4}$ you can usually hear pretty easily where the first beat is: It sounds or feels a little stronger than the rest, which is why it's known as a *strong beat* or a *natural accent*. The third beat, though slightly less strong, is also referred to as a natural accent. Two and four are the *weak beats*.

Downbeat

Other names for the first and third beats are *accented beats*, *principal metric accents*, or *downbeats*. The last term automatically turns beats two and four into upbeats or *offbeats*.

Pop, rock, jazz

In most pop and rock tunes, the snare drum clearly accents the 'weak' second and fourth beats. Played that way, they're referred to as *afterbeats* or *backbeats*. The first and third beats, however, still tend to feel stronger. No matter how loud the drummer is banging out 2 and 4, some audiences still tend to clap along on 1 and 3.

Meter

The term *meter* is closely related to what you know as *time signature*, although it is not exactly the same. The time signature specifies both the number of beats per bar and the kind of beats (the counting unit: quarter notes, or eighth notes, and so on) The meter only indicates the number of beats. *Quadruple meter* means four beats per bar. In *triple meter* there are three, and in *duple meter* there are two beats or *units* per bar.

Simple and compound meters

Duple, triple, and quadruple meter are also known as *common meter* or *simple meter*. If you multiply common meters by three, you get *compound meters* (*e.g.*, ⁶⁄₈ or ⁹⁄₈).

Two groups of three: ⁶⁄₄ and ⁶⁄₈   Tipcode MOP-049

In pieces in ⁶⁄₄ and ⁶⁄₈, each bar is usually felt as two groups of three notes. You don't count ⁶⁄₈ as 1, 2, 3, 4, 5, 6, but you count two beats instead. Each beat equals a dotted quarter note, which can be divided into three (three eighth notes) – a characteristic of compound time.

Two groups of three in every bar: a melody in ⁶⁄₈.

ODD TIME SIGNATURES

Irregular or *odd time signatures* have an odd number of beats, such as ⁵⁄₄ or ¹¹⁄₈. Odd time signatures are quite uncommon in Western music.

Counting in groups   Tipcode MOP-050

Odd time signatures are usually counted in subgroups. For example, ⁵⁄₄ can be counted as 1, 2, 3, 1, 2, or the other way around, as 1, 2, 1, 2, 3. Which one you choose depends on the division of strong and weak beats in the piece.

Take Five

One of the few really well-known pieces in ⁵⁄₄ is the jazz standard 'Take Five,' written in the late 1950s. In this piece, the strong beats are on 1 and 4, dividing each bar up into a first subgroup of three notes, and a second subgroup of two notes (1, 2, 3, 1, 2).

CHAPTER 16

Tune in $\frac{5}{4}$.

SWING

The word *swing* is used mostly in jazz. In swing style, eighth notes are played and felt more as triplets than as regular, 'straight' eighth notes: The music has a *triplet feel*.

In eighths
Tipcode MOP-051

The parts that jazz players use, however, show normal eighth notes. To indicate that they're to be played with a triplet or swing feel, these parts may either show the word 'swing,' or you'll see the following indication:

Play the eighth notes with a triplet feel.

Straight eighths

Some pieces have sections that you play as swing, and others where you have to play straight eighth notes. The latter sections are then indicated with the words *straight eighths*, *even eighths*, or *even 8ths*.

AND MORE...

In most pop, rock, and classical music, the accented beats are governed by the time signature: There are one or more accents in each bar, usually on the first and third beat.

Syncopation

Especially in jazz, these accents are often hidden. Instead, other notes are accented, such as the eighth note after a beat. This is known as *syncopation*.

The clave
Tipcode MOP-052

There's also music where the main accents make up a pattern that is spread over two or more bars. A lot of Latin American music, for example, is based on the *clave*, a rhythmic pattern that has five accents over two bars. It may be played as shown below (the 2-3 clave), or the other way around, starting on the second bar (3-2 clave).

The 2-3 clave: five accents spread out over two bars.

Changing time signature

In some music, the time signature changes one or more times throughout the piece, and composers can use an endless variety of irregular meters, such as $\frac{9}{16}$ or $\frac{13}{8}$. These and other complicated time signatures are often used in twentieth-century classical music, Arabic music, and sometimes in fusion, for example.

Polyrhythm

Polyrhythm is playing different, contrasting rhythms simultaneously. This is often done in jazz soloing, for example, but there are polyrhythmic compositions too, and polyrhythm is very common in traditional African music. A simple example of a polyrhythm is playing two against three: quarter notes against one quarter-note triplet. (Two quarter notes equal one quarter-note triplet.)

17. DO, RE, MI – I, II, III

In Chapter 2, the octave was illustrated using the sequence *do, re, mi, fa, so, la, ti, do*. These syllables are another way of indicating notes. A third way is to use Roman numerals.

The sequence *do, re, mi*, etc., is used in two ways: either with a *permanent do* or *fixed do*, where *do* always represents C, or with a *movable do*.

Major scale
The movable *do* stands for the first note of a (major) scale: the root or tonic. If you sing *do, re, mi*, etc., starting on an A, you'll be singing the scale of A-major. And if you start on a C♯, you'll be singing the scale of C♯ major.

The fixed *do*
In some countries, such as France and Spain, *do* always represents C. For example, C-major is known in France as *do Majeur*.

Solmization
This system of indicating notes with syllables is known as *solmization*, and it's also referred to as *solfege*.

Black notes
The system includes names for the half steps too.
• When a note is raised the name is pronounced with an *i* sound, just like the syllables indicating the two half steps in the major scale (*mi* and *ti*, pronounced as *mee* and *tee*): *do, di, re, ri, mi, fa, fi, so, si, la, li, ti, do*.

- Lowered note names use an *a* sound: *do, ra, re, me, mi, fa, se, so, le, la, te, ti, do*.

Trick
You can use these sequences to figure out the notes of a scale. If you want to find out the scale of A-major, jot down the chromatic scale of A under the *do-re-mi* scale, and see which notes line up with the syllables *do, re, mi*, and so on: that's A-major.

do	di	re	ri	mi	fa	fi	so	si	la	li	ti	do
A	A♯	B	C	C♯	D	D♯	E	F	F♯	G	G♯	A

Flats
You can use the same trick for scales that have one or more flats in the key signature, such as F-major.

do	ra	re	me	mi	fa	se	so	le	la	te	ti	do
F	G♭	G	A♭	A	B♭	B	C	D♭	D	E♭	E	F

I, II, III
The system of indicating notes by using Roman numerals is quite similar. The first eight numerals (I, II, III, IV, V, VI, VII, VIII) represent the major scale. Instead of Roman numerals, some prefer to use 'regular' numbers (1, 2 , etc.).

Numerals	I	II	III	IV	V	VI	VII	VIII
Syllables	do	re	mi	fa	so	la	ti	do
Steps	first	second	third	fourth	fifth	sixth	seventh	eighth

Flats and sharps
To create a chromatic scale the familiar sharps and flats are used. Flats are usually written before the numeral they refer to (*i.e,* ♭V), and sharps afterward (i.e., IV♯).

do	di	re	ri	mi	fa	fi	so	si	la	li	ti	do
I	I♯	II	II♯	III	IV	IV♯	V	V♯	VI	VI♯	VII	VIII

do	di	re	ri	mi	fa	fi	so	si	la	ii	ti	do
I	♭II	II	♭III	III	IV	♭V	V	♭VI	VI	♭VII	VII	VIII

18. CHORDS, TAB, AND DRUM MUSIC

The standard system of music notation as explained in this book allows you to write down almost everything you can play. But in some styles and for some instruments different ways of notation are used.

In pop, jazz, and related styles, the melody is notated on a regular staff; the accompanying chords are shown as chord symbols.

Chord symbol	Alternative symbols	Notes
C		C, E, G
Cm	C–, Cmi, Cmin	C, E♭, G
Caug5	C+5, C♯5	C, E, G♯
Cdim	C°	C, E♭, G♭
C♭5		C, E, G♭
C7	Cdom7	C, E, G, B♭
Cmaj7	CM7, CΔ, CΔ7	C, E, G, B
C6	Cmaj6	C, E, G, A
C7♭9	C7–9	C, E, G, B♭, D♭
C9		C, E, G, B♭, D
Cm7	Cmi7, Cmin7, C–7	C, E♭, G, B♭
Cdim	C°	C, E♭, G♭, A
Cm6	Cmin6, C-6	C, E♭, G, A
Cm7♭5	Cm7♭5, C-7♭5, Cø7	C, E♭, G♭, B♭
Cmima7	Cm(maj7), CmΔ7, C-Δ	C, E♭, G, B
Csus4		C, F, G

Chord symbols

The letter in a chord symbol represents the root note or tonic of the chord. Numbers and abbreviations tell you which other notes to play. Sharps, flats and other symbols give additional information. The table below shows some of the most frequently used chord symbols, including some alternative notations. Like elsewhere in this book, the key of C is used as an example.

All musicians

The chord symbols tell keyboard players, pianists, and guitarists which chords to play, but they also tell all musicians which notes to use in a solo, and they tell bass players which notes they can use for their bass lines

Another bass note

Bassists can be directed to play another note than the root of the chord. Cmaj7/E, for example, is a C-major seven chord with an E as the bass note (rather than the C).

Inversions Tipcode MOP-053

The notes in a chord can be shuffled in various ways; these

Steps (numerals)	Steps (roman numerals)	Referred to as
1, 3, 5	I, III, V	C-major
1, ♭3, 5	I, ♭III, V	C-minor
1, 3, 5♯	I, III, V♯	C augmented
1, ♭3, ♭5	I, ♭III, ♭V	C diminished
1, 3, ♭5	I, III, ♭V	C flattened five
1, 3, 5, ♭7	I, III, V, ♭VII	C seven
1, 3, 5, 7	I, III, V, VII	C-major seven
1, 3, 5, 6	I, III, V, VI	C six
1, 3, 5, ♭7, ♭9	I, III, V, ♭VI, ♭IX	C seven flat nine
1, 3, 5, ♭7, 9	I, III, V, ♭VI, IX	C nine
1, ♭3, 5, ♭7	I, ♭III, V, ♭VII	C-minor seven
1, ♭3, ♭5, 6	I, ♭II, ♭V, VI	C diminished
1, ♭3, 5, 6	I, ♭III, V, VI	C-minor six
1, ♭3, ♭5, ♭7	I, ♭III, ♭V, ♭VII	C half diminished – C-minor flat five
1, ♭3, 5, 7	I, ♭III, V, VII	C-minor/major seven
1, 4, 5	I, IV, V	C suspended

variations are referred to as inversions. The following diagram shows two examples of a popular chord sequence (a II-V-I progression). Inverting the middle chord makes this progression both easier to play and easier to the ear.

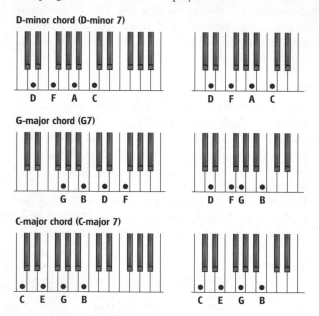

First play the left-hand chord sequence, top to bottom; then play the right-hand sequence and hear the effect of the inverted middle chord (G7).

Chord voicing
The notes in a chord can be stacked upon one another in various different ways, or voicings, as felt by the player to best suit the music. Often the 5th, the 7th, or other notes are omitted, if they're not required to convey the harmony. For example, a C9♯11 chord could be voiced as C–E–G–B♭–D–F♯, but you could also play it as C–B♭–D–F♯ or C–D–F♯–B♭. Selecting appropriate, effective, and interesting chordal voicings is an art that demands good ears and a lot of practice.

CHORD CHARTS AND TABLATURE
For guitarists, chords can be displayed as chord charts. The tablature system can be used to put solos and melodies on paper.

Chord charts

A chord chart is a diagram showing a part of the guitar's fingerboard with the strings and the frets. Dots tell you where to put your fingers.

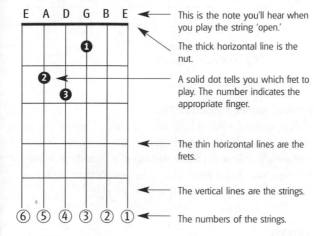

E A D G B E ← This is the note you'll hear when you play the string 'open.'

← The thick horizontal line is the nut.

← A solid dot tells you which fret to play. The number indicates the appropriate finger.

← The thin horizontal lines are the frets.

← The vertical lines are the strings.

⑥ ⑤ ④ ③ ② ① ← The numbers of the strings.

Put your index finger (1) on string 3 in the first position, your middle finger (2) on string 5 in the second position, and your ring finger (3) on string 4 in the second position. This is an E-major chord.

Chord books and digital devices

Chord charts are often included in rock and pop sheet music, but separate books showing a multitude of different chords and inversions are also available, as well as handy digital alternatives. Similar devices are available for keyboardists and pianists as well, indicating how to play each chord on a keyboard instrument.

Tablature

The tablature or tab system allows you to read guitar solos, melodies, and bass lines without using standard notation. Tablature shows you exactly in which order to put which fingers on which strings.

The strings   Tipcode MOP-054

Similar to chord charts, the six lines of a tab staff represent the strings of your guitar. The numbers on the strings tell you at which frets you should stop them; the numbers below suggest which finger to use.

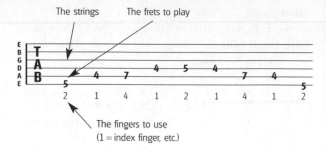

The strings   The frets to play

The fingers to use
(1 = index finger, etc.)

The tablature staff represents a guitar neck.

Standard notation included

Tablature doesn't show how long the notes should last, or when to play them: The rhythm is not indicated. That's why song books with tablature usually include standard notation too. If you know the song, you will usually know the rhythm – so you can rely on tab only.

DRUMS
Tipcode MOP-055

Music for drummers is written on a regular five-line staff. The notes, however, don't indicate various pitches, but the various parts of the drum set. As the drum set is not a standardized instrument, drum set notation isn't very standardized either. The basic parts of the drum set, however, are usually written as shown below. Toms sit in the spaces or on the lines above and below the snare drum. Crash cymbals are often indicated on a ledger line above the staff. There's a variety of ways to indicate special effects and sounds such as rimshots (hitting a drum on the head and the hoop simultaneously) and rimclicks (playing the rim with the other end of the stick resting on the head).

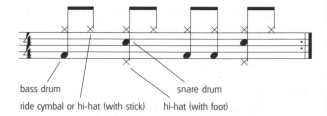

bass drum   snare drum
ride cymbal or hi-hat (with stick)   hi-hat (with foot)

A basic rock rhythm in drum set notation.

19. PUTTING NOTES TO PAPER

If you can read music, you can also write it. Writing it down is easier than remembering it – whether it's a tune you just thought up, an idea for a solo, or an entire symphony. Writing music is good practice too: Writing out scales, for example, is one of the most effective ways to really get to know and understand them.

To put music on paper, you can get pre-printed music paper in most music stores. A pencil (with eraser) is usually easiest for sketches. Use a pen or a fineliner for the final version.

- Making perfectly even, round, or oval heads by hand is very difficult. A good alternative is to draw the heads of the closed notes (quarters, eighths) **as thick, short slashes**.

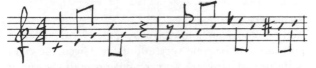

Note heads are often drawn as slashes.

- In single-voice melodies **the stems of notes** above the third (middle) line are at the left side of the note, pointing down. For notes lower down on the staff, the rule is reversed: The note-stem is on the right side, pointing up. In writing notes *on* the third line (B, in the treble clef), what you do depends on whether the melody is going up or down. If you group a number of notes including some above and some below the third line, you can do it as you please.
- If you want to combine **two melodies on one staff**, then write the lower one with all stems pointing down, and

the other one with all stems pointing up.
- **Flags** are always drawn on the right of the stem.
  - • Writing a correct **quarter rest** becomes easy if you think of it as a tilted Z over a capital C.
- Draw **sharps and flats** on the same level as the heads of the notes to which they apply.
- There's no easy way to draw a **treble clef**. You'll just have to practice.
- Use **beams** if you divide a beat up into eighth or sixteenth notes.
- Reading is easier if every bar has **the same length**. As a rule of thumb, you can divide every staff into four equal bars.
- Make sure you **don't have bars spilling** over to the next lines.
- If you write for a keyboard player or pianist, make sure to **align the notes** in the treble and bass staffs.

The rhythm of each part should be aligned correctly.

Computers

You can also score music on a computer. Music notation software has become very affordable. Given the right software and hardware, your computer may also be a great help in a lot of other things, such as transposing at the touch of a button, or playing back the music you've been writing. This may be less instructive than doing it by hand, but it's very fast and effective.

MIDI

Home keyboards, synthesizers, and other electronic instruments can be hooked up to your computer using a system called MIDI (Musical Instruments Digital Interface). An appropriate soundcard and additional software is required for this purpose. This allows you to record on your hard disk and to edit the results, to score music by simply playing it 'into' your computer, or to play back files using the instrument as a sound source. The possibilities are endless, as you can read in any of the many books on this subject.

20. BACK IN TIME

Music notation wasn't invented in one beat. Like most musical instruments, it evolved, step by step. This chapter takes a quick look at its history, from neums to notes, and from lines to staves.

Pythagoras is credited with creating the chromatic scale, which divides the octave into twelve equal steps, around 2,500 years ago. About a thousand years later these notes were given their letter names.

Written music

Some of the oldest surviving examples of written Western music are the Gregorian chants, named after Pope Gregory the Great (540–604). Little marks (*neums*) were added to the texts of these chants to indicate the direction of the melody.

Lines

Some four centuries later, a single line was used to indicate a particular pitch. The invention of the four-line staff, in the first half of the eleventh century, is attributed to the Italian monk Guido of Arezzo (c. 991– c. 1050). Modern notes and rests can already be recognized in manuscripts dating from that time. The five-line staff has been common since the thirteenth century, and musical notation has

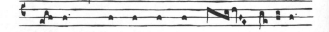

A four-line staff with Gregorian music.

remained basically unchanged since the seventeenth century.

Ut, re, mi

To make learning to read music a bit easier, Guido of Arezzo paired syllables with the various pitches, using the words from a hymn to Saint John. The result was the sequence *ut, re, mi, fa, sol, la.*

The hymn to Saint John.

Do, re, mi

Around 1600, a seventh note (*si*) was added to this sequence, now covering the entire major scale: *ut, re, mi, fa, sol, la, si, ut,* in which *si* is short for Sancte Ioannes (Saint John). Later, *sol* became *so, si* became *ti,* and the church changed the syllable *ut* to *do,* saying that God (*Do*minum) was the root – the beginning and the end – of all things.

Italian

The Roman Catholic Church, ruled from the Vatican in Rome, has always had a lot of influence on music history. Over the centuries it issued all sorts of rules and guidelines, covering pretty much every aspect from notation to composition. This is one reason why you come across so many Italian words and abbreviations in sheet music.

SIGNS AND MARKINGS

Below you'll find all the signs and markings covered in this book. The number between parentheses refers to the page where you can find more information.

RHYTHM

	bar line (15)
$\frac{4}{4}$	time signature (18)
C	common time (19)
¢	alla breve (20)
⌐3⌐ / ⌐3⌐	triplet bracket (24)
·	dot (23)
⌣	tie (23)
♩=120	metronome marking (39)

LOUD AND SOFT

p	piano (36)
pp	pianissimo (36)
ppp	pianississimo (36)
mp	mezzo-piano (36)
mf	mezzo-forte (36)
f	forte (36)
ff	fortissimo (36)
fff	fortississimo (36)
sf sfz	sforzando (37)
fp	fortepiano (37)
<	crescendo (37)
>	decrescendo (37)

PITCH

𝄞	treble clef or G-clef (10)
𝄢	bass clef or F-clef (10)
𝄡	C-clef (11)
♯	sharp (27)
♭	flat (27)
𝄪	double sharp (35)
♭♭	double flat (35)
♮	natural (33)

REPEAT AND SECTION

	repeat sign (52)
·/·	repeat previous bar (52)
·//·	repeat previous two bars (52)
/	repeat previous chord (56)
𝄋	segno (54)
⊕	coda sign (54)
1 2	first and second ending (58)
	section line (52)
	double bar line (57)
C	rehearsal mark (51)
25	bar number (52)

ORNAMENTATION

tr	trill (47)
♦	mordent (47)
	inverted mordent (48)
♮ *trem.*	tremolo (48)
♪	grace note or appoggiatura (49)
∞	turn (49)
	glissando (50)
	fall (50)
	lift (50)
	plop (50)
	doit (50)

ARTICULATION

⌢	phrase mark (44)
⌣	slur (44)
⌢	fermata (45)
>	accent (43)
∧	intense accent (43)
	tenuto (45)
·	staccato (43)
▲	staccatissimo (44)
♩♩ ↑₀	du-wah (46)
⌣	scoop (46)
×	ghost note (46)

GLOSSARY AND INDEX

This glossary gives a short definition of all the terms and abbreviations mentioned in this book. The numbers refer to the page(s) where the subject is addressed in more detail. This list also contains a few words you will not find in this book, but which you could come across in certain pieces.

A tempo *(41)* Go back to the original tempo, after a quicker or a slower section. Also indicated as *Tempo I°* ('Tempo Primo').

Accelerando, Acc. *(41)* Get faster.

Accent *(43, 44, 45)* Makes a note sound slightly louder.

Accidentals *(31, 33–34, 35)* Sharps and flats that are not in the key signature, or natural signs.

Ad libitum *(41)* Literally: 'at liberty' or 'as you please'. Often abbreviated to *ad lib.*

Adagio *(40)* Tempo mark. Slow; metronome marking 60–76.

Aeolian mode *(88)* Traditional mode, also known as A-mode. Similar to the minor scale. See: *Traditional modes* and *Minor, minor scale.*

Agitato *(42)* Agitated.

Al coda *(54–55)* See: *Coda.*

Al fine *(54)* To the end. Often used in combination with Da Capo (from the beginning).

Alla breve *(20)* *Cut common time* or $\frac{2}{2}$. Indicated using the symbol ₵.

Allargando *(41)* Literally: 'broadening out': get slower and a little louder.

Allegro, Allegretto, Allegrissimo *(40)* Tempo marks.

Alto clef *(12)* C clef, indicating Middle C on the third line. Also see: *Clef.*

Andante *(40)* Tempo mark.

Appoggiatura See: *Grace note.*

Articulation markings *(43–46)* Markings that indicate how to 'pronounce' a note (long, short, bold, broad, and so on).

Assai *(42)* Literally: 'very' or 'sufficient.' Used in combination with other indications. See: *Tempo markings*.

Augmented *(75)* An augmented interval is a major or perfect interval enlarged by a half step. C–F is a perfect fourth, C–F♯ is an augmented fourth. See: *Interval*, *Major*, and *Perfect*.

B♭ instruments *(92)* See: *Transposing instruments*.

Backbeat *(96)* Term used especially in rock and pop music. The drummer hits the snare drum on the backbeat – usually the second and fourth beats in four-four.

Bar, bar line *(15, 18–20)* Music is divided into bars or measures using vertical lines (*bar* lines) drawn on the staff.

Bass clef *(10)* Another name for the F-clef. See also: *Clef*.

Beams *(20–21)* Replace flags; used to group eighth, sixteenth, and shorter notes that make up one beat.

Beats per minute *(39–40)* Often abbreviated to BPM. The number of beats per minute indicate the tempo of a piece. See: *Metronome marking*.

Black note *(7)* The black keys on a keyboard instrument are also referred to as black notes. See: *White key, white note*.

Blues scale *(91)* The classic blues scale is made up of whole steps, half steps, and two intervals of a step and a half (a minor third). See: *Interval*.

BPM See: *Beats per minute*.

Bridge *(51, 55)* The bridge or *chorus* bridges two sections of a piece.

C-clef *(11–12)* See: *Clef*.

Capo *(54)* The beginning. See: *Da Capo* and *Al Fine*.

Chart See: *Part*.

Chord *(13–14, 102–104)* Three or more notes played simultaneously.

Chord charts *(104–105)* Enable you to write and read guitar chords without using staff notation.

Chorus See: *Bridge*.

Chromatic scale *(90)* Scale made up of twelve half steps.

Chromatic signs See: *Sharp*, *Flat*, and *Natural symbol*.

Church modes See: *Traditional modes*.

Circle of fifths *(69–72, 84)* A circle containing all major *(71)* and relative minor scales *(84)*, including the number of sharps or flats in each scale.

Clave *(98)* The rhythmic basis for many types of Latin American music.

Clef *(10–13)* Symbol that specifies the pitch of a particular line on a staff, and thus the pitches of all other lines and spaces. The two most common clefs are the *G-clef* or *treble clef* and the *F-clef* or *bass clef*. The C-clef is a *moveable clef*.

Coda *(54–55)* The 'tail' or the end of a piece. Also known as *postlude* or '*outro*.'

Common meter See: *Simple meter*.

Common time *(19)* Four-four time or $\frac{4}{4}$ time signature. See: *Four-four time*, *Time signature*, and *Meter*.

Compound meter *(97)* See: *Simple meter*.

Con brio, con fuoco, con spirito *(42)* With brilliance, with fire (*fuoco*), spirited, with vigor.

Consonant *(77–78)* Literally: 'sounding (well) together.' Consonant intervals are divided up into *perfect* and *imperfect consonants*. See also: *Dissonant*.

Counting unit *(19)* Lower number in the time signature. You can see from the counting unit which note duration is counted, or, in other words, which note duration is equal to one beat. See: *Time signature* and *Meter*.

Crescendo *(37)* Get louder.

Cut common time See: *Alla breve*.

Da Capo *(54–55)* Play again from the beginning.

Dal Segno, D.S. *(54)* 'From the sign.' From the bar where D.S. is indicated, go back to the sign $\%$ (*segno*).

Decrescendo *(37)* Get softer.

Degree See: *Step*.

Diatonic scales *(89)* Diatonic scales consist of two half steps and five whole steps. The traditional modes are diatonic.

Diminished interval *(75)* A perfect interval which has been reduced by a half step.

Diminuendo *(37)* Get softer.

Dissonant *(77–78)* 'Not sounding (well) together'. Intervals are divided in dissonant and consonant intervals. See also: *Consonant*.

Do-re-mi *(6, 100–101, 111)* Sequence of syllables, representing a scale.

Doit *(50)* Ornament: a short upward bend of the note.

Dolce *(42)* Sweetly, lovely.

Dorian *(88)* Traditional mode, also known as D-mode.

Dot, dotted *(23–24)* A dot after a note (a dotted note) means that it lasts one and a half times as long.

Double bar line *(52)* Double vertical line, one thin, one thick. Marks the end of a piece.

Double flat *(35)* Indicated by ♭♭: This note is lowered by two half steps. See: *Flat*.

Double sharp *(35)* Indicated by 𝄪. This note is raised by two half steps. See: *Sharp*.

Downbeat See: *Natural accents*.

Du-wah *(46)* Ornament, mainly used by mouth harp and trumpet players.

Dur *(80)* Another name for major. See: *Major scale*.

Dynamic markings *(36–38)* Signs and abbreviations that show how loudly or softly a piece should be played.

E♭ instruments See: *Transposing instruments*.

Enharmonic *(34, 65, 72, 75)* Sounds the same, but called by different names, whether applied to intervals, notes, or scales.

F-clef *(10)* Alternative name for the bass clef. See: *Clef*.

Fall *(50)* Ornament.

Fermata *(45)* A note of indefinite length. Also known as *pause*.

Fifth *(74)* Interval of five steps (*e.g.*, C to G).

Fine *(54)* Finish, end. This

116

is where it really stops. See: *Al Fine*.

First ending *(53)* When a section of music is repeated, the ending is often different the second time around. These different endings are marked as *first* and *second endings*.

Flat *(27–35)* 1. Symbol (♭) indicating that a note must be lowered by one half step. 2. Too low. A guitar string that sounds flat should be tuned up.

Forte *(f)*, **fortissimo** *(ff)*, **fortississimo** *(fff)* *(36)* Loud, very loud, as loud as possible.

Forte-piano *(fp)* *(36)* Loud, followed immediately by soft.

Four-four time *(49)* *Common time* or $\frac{4}{4}$.

Fourth *(74)* Interval of four steps (*e.g.*, C to F).

G-clef *(10)* Alternative name for treble clef. See: *Clef*.

Ghost note *(46)* Ornament. Smothered, 'dead' note.

Gypsy scale *(91)* Scale with an interval of one-and-a-half steps in two places.

Glissando *(50)* Ornament. Slide from one note to the next.

Grace note *(49)* Ornament: a 'small' note immediately preceding the main one. Also known as *appoggiatura*.

Grupetto See: *Turn*.

Half step *(7, 58–59)* A minor *second*; the smallest distance between two notes in Western music (*e.g.*, from C to C♯). Also referred to as *half tone* or *semitone*.

Half tone See: *Half step*.

Harmonic minor *(82–83)* Alteration of the minor scale; has a raised seventh step.

Hexatonic scale *(90)* See: *Whole tone scale*.

High C Depends on the instrument or voice type. For a tenor voice, high C is C5. For a soprano, it's C6. Some call C6 *double-high C*.

Home note See: *Root*.

Imperfect consonant See: *Consonant*.

Interlude *(51)* An interlude joins two different parts of a piece. See also: *Bridge*.

Interval *(73–79)* The distance from one note to another.

Inverted mordent *(48)* Short trill to the note below the main note.

Ionian *(88)* Traditional mode, also known as C-mode. Similar to the major scale. See: *Traditional modes* and *Major scale*.

Irregular time signature See: *Odd time signature*.

Key *(32, 57, 60, 65, 68)* The key refers to the scale that a piece of music is based on. If a piece is in A-major, it is based on the scale of A-major.

Key note See: *Root*.

Key signature *(32–33, 34, 64–68, 83, 84)* The sharp(s) or flat(s) at the beginning of a staff. Tells you the key the piece is in, and which note(s) to raise or to lower.

Largo, Larghetto *(40)* Very slow (metronome marking 40–60), a little less slow (metronome marking 60–66).

Leading note, leading tone *(81)* Note that leads to the root or home note. Also known as *subtonic*.

Ledger lines *(12)* Short lines drawn above and below the staff, used to extend its range. (See: *Range*).

Legato *(44)* 'Bound'. When playing legato, each note flows into the next one.

Lento Slow, dragging.

Lift *(50)* Ornament: slide up to the note.

Loco *(12)* Ends a section that's marked to be played one or two octaves higher or lower.

Locrian *(88)* Traditional mode, also known as B-mode. See: *Traditional modes*.

Lydian *(88)* Traditional mode, also known as F-mode. See: *Traditional modes*.

Major See: *Major scale*. Also: qualifying indication for intervals (major second, third, sixth, and seventh). See: *Interval*.

Major scale *(58–66, 71, 80)* Scale with whole (W) and half (H) steps in the following order: W, W, H, W, W, W, H. Similar to the Ionian mode. See: *Minor, minor scale*.

Marcato *(43)* 'Marked'. The notes in a marcato passage must be given extra emphasis.

Measure See: *Bar.*

Melodic minor *(81–82)* Alteration of the minor scale; the sixth and seventh steps are raised.

Meno *(42)* Less.

Meter *(96)* Measurement of time in music. The meter of a piece indicates the number of beats assigned to each measure or bar. In quadruple meter every bar has four beats.

Metronome *(39–40)* Electronic or mechanical device that indicates the tempo with ticks, beeps, or flashes.

Metronome marking *(39–40, 41–42)* Indicates how fast a piece must be played, expressed in the number of beats per minute (BPM).

Mezzo forte *(mf)*, **mezzo piano** *(mp)* *(36)* Moderately loud, moderately soft.

Middle C *(8)* The C written on the ledger line between the treble and bass clefs. On a piano, Middle C is in the middle of the keyboard.

Minor, minor scale *(60, 66–67, 71, 80)* Scale with whole (W) and half (H) steps in the following order: W, H, W, W, H, W, W. Compared to a major scale, the third, sixth, and seventh steps are flattened (*e.g.*, C, D, E♭, F, G, A♭, B♭, C). A minor chord has a flattened third (*e.g.*, C, E♭, G).

Minor interval *(75)* Reduced major interval.

Mixolydian *(88)* Traditional mode, also known as G-mode.

Modal music *(89)* Music that's based on the structure of a certain *mode*. See: *Mode.*

Mode *(80)* Means 'way'. Used to indicate scales (*e.g.*, traditional modes).

Moderato *(40)* Medium tempo: not too fast, not too slow (metronome marking 108-120).

Modulation *(67–68)* To move from one key to another.

Moll *(80)* Another name for minor. See: *Minor scale.*

Molto *(42)* Italian for 'very'.

Mordent *(47–48)* Short

trill to the note above the main note.

Movable *do* *(100)* The movable *do* represents the root of a scale. See: *do, re, mi.*

Natural 1. *(7, 94)* The naturals or natural notes are the notes sounded by the white keys of a keyboard instrument. Also called white notes. See: *White key, white note.* 2. *(33)* Sign indicating that a sharp or flat, either in the key signature or as an accidental within the music, must be (temporarily) cancelled: ♮.

Natural accents *(96)* In ⁴⁄₄, beats 1 and (to a lesser extent) 3 are naturally accented. In ⁶⁄₈, the first and fourth beats have a natural accent. Also known as *strong beats*, (*principal*) *metric accents, accented beats*, or *downbeats*. The second and fourth beat in ⁴⁄₄ are known as the *weak beats, unaccented beats*, or *upbeats*.

Natural minor *(83)* The regular, unaltered minor scale, also known *original minor*. See: *Harmonic minor, Melodic minor.*

Non troppo *(42)* Italian for 'not too much.'

Non-diatonic See: *Diatonic scales.*

Note *(16–17)* Can be written or sounded. The look of a note tells how long it's supposed to last. There are whole, half, quarter, eighth, and shorter notes.

Note value *(18)* The length of a note.

Octatonic scale *(90)* A scale made up of alternating half and whole steps.

Octave *(6, 8, 73–74)* Interval that spans eight white notes on a piano keyboard.

Odd time signature *(97–98)* Time signature in which the beats in each bar are subdivided into unequal groups (*e.g.*, ⁵⁄₄, divided into 2+3 or 3+2).

Original minor See: *Natural minor.*

Ornamentations *(47–50)* Various symbols used to indicate that a note should be embellished with extra notes or trills.

Outro See: *Coda.*

Parallel *(84–85)* Keys with the same root are parallel keys, *e.g.*, C-major and C-minor.

Pause See: *Fermata.*

Pentatonic scales *(90)* Pentatonic scales are made up of five notes (*penta* = five).

Perfect *(75)* Extra indication for certain intervals (perfect unison, fourth and fifth, and perfect octave).

Perfect consonant See: *Consonant.*

Phrase mark *(44)* Curved line indicating that a group of notes (a phrase) belong together.

Phrygian *(88)* Traditional mode, also known as E-mode.

Piano (*p*), **pianissimo** (*pp*), **pianissississimo** (*ppp*) *(36)* Soft, very soft, as soft as possible.

Pickup *(26)* Usually an incomplete bar at the beginning of a piece. Also called *upbeat.*

Pitch bend *(50)* 'Bending' the pitch of a note up or down.

Più *(42)* Italian for 'more'.

Pizzicato *(45)* If a violinist plays pizzicato, the strings are plucked, not bowed.

See: *Articulation markings.*

Plop *(50)* Ornament. 'Falling into the note.'

Poco, poco a poco *(41)* Italian for 'a little,' 'gradually' or 'bit by bit.'

Portato See: *Tenuto.*

Postlude See: *Coda.*

Presto, prestissimo *(42)* Fast (metronome marking 176–200), very fast (metronome marking 200 or more).

Quintuplet *(26)* A note divided into five equal parts.

Rallentando, rall. *(41)* Get slower.

Relative major, relative minor *(83–85)* Major and minor keys with the same key signature.

Reminder accidentals *(34)* Sharp, flat, or natural signs that remind you that an accidental indicated earlier still applies. See: *Accidentals.*

Repeat signs *(52–53, 56)* Repeat signs indicate that one or more bars should be repeated.

Rests *(22)* Moments of silence in music.

Ritardando, rit., ritard., ritenuto, riten. *(41)* Get slower.

Root, root note *(58, 59, 60, 77)* Also known as tonic, home note, or key note. It's the first (and last) note of a scale. Most pieces end on the root of the key in which they are written.

Rubato *(40)* Free tempo. In parts marked rubato you can't tap along with your foot: There is no set tempo.

Scale *(57–58, 60–67)* Series of at least five notes, arranged low to high. The key signature and the root of a piece tell you which scale it is based on.

Scoop *(49)* Slight bend in the note, from the main note down and then back. See: *Ornament*.

Score *(4)* Usually refers to a book of music containing the parts of all musicians in a piece. *To score* means either to put notes to paper or to arrange a work for different instruments.

Second *(74)* Interval of two steps (*e.g.*, C to D).

Second ending See: *First ending*.

Section line *(52)* Double vertical (bar) line that groups two or more bars into sections.

Section markings *(51–52)* Musical signposts that indicate the various parts of a piece.

Segno *(54)* The Segno symbol 𝄋 indicates that you must jump to the coda. See: *Coda* and *Dal Segno*.

Semitone See: *Half step*.

Septuplet *(26)* A note divided into seven equal parts.

Seventh *(74)* Interval of seven steps (*e.g.*, C to B).

Sextuplet *(25)* A note divided into six equal parts.

Sforzando (sf or sfz) *(37)* Loud and then immediately soft. This symbol is often followed by a crescendo. See: *Crescendo*.

Sharp 1. *(27–35)* Symbol (♯) indicating that a note must be raised by one half step. 2. Sharp also means 'too high in pitch,' as opposed to flat. See: *Flat*.

Simile *(45)* Keep playing the same way. Keep playing

staccato notes, for example.

Simple meter *(97)* $\frac{2}{4}$, $\frac{3}{4}$, and $\frac{4}{4}$ are examples of simple or *common meter*. In compound meter, each bar is usually subdivided in two or more groups (*e.g.*, $\frac{6}{8}$ or $\frac{12}{8}$).

Sixth *(74)* Interval of six steps (*e.g.*, C to A).

Slur *(44)* A curved line, indicating that a group of notes should be played legato. Not to be confused with a *tie*.

Staccato, staccatissimo *(43–44)* Short, very short.

Staff *(8–9)* The five horizontal lines used for the notation of music. Staffs can be enlarged using ledger lines. Sometimes spelled as *stave*.

Step 1. *(69, 70)* A certain note in a scale or mode. The second step or *degree* of a scale is the second note of that scale. 2. Another word for tone: A whole step equals a whole tone (*e.g.*, C-D). See also: *Whole step*.

Straight eighths *(98)* Also known as *even eighths*. The 'opposite' of swing. See: *Swing*.

Stringendo, string. *(41)*

'Urgently'. Get a bit faster and louder.

Subtonic See: *Leading note*.

Swing *(98)* The word 'swing' at the beginning of a piece tells you to play the eighth notes in a way that's commonly known as a *triplet feel*, as opposed to playing them as regular *straight eighths*: *daate-daate-daate-daate* rather than daadaa-daadaa-daadaa-daadaa.

Tablature *(105–106)* System of writing parts for guitarists, keyboard players, and other musicians, based on chord indications rather than notes.

Tail See: *Coda*.

Tempo *(39–42)* The speed at which a piece is played.

Tempo markings *(39–42)* tell you how fast a piece must be played. Indicated with Italian words or numbers. See: *Metronome marking*.

Tempo primo, tempo I° See: *A Tempo*.

Tenor clef *(12)* C clef,

indicating Middle C on the fourth line. See also: *Clef*.

Tenuto *(45)* Notes with a tenuto mark should sound for their full duration, without joining them together. The same mark is also referred to as *portato* (stately, solemn).

Tetrachord *(89)* The two halves of a diatonic scale.

Third *(74)* Interval of three steps (*e.g.*, C to E).

Three-four time *(19)* A piece in three-four time ($\frac{3}{4}$) has three quarter notes in every bar. See: *Time signatures*, *Meter*, and *Counting unit*.

Tie *(23–24)* Curved line tying notes of the same pitch to each other.

Time signature *(18–20, 96)* The time signature, given at the beginning of a piece or a section, indicates the counting unit (lower number) and how many beats or counts there are in each bar (the upper number).

Tone 1. Another word for step (see: *Step*). 2. The tone or *timbre* of an instrument refers to the character of its sound.

Tonic See: *Root*.

Traditional modes *(88–89)* Seven modes or scales that can be played with the white notes on a keyboard. Also known as *church modes*.

Tranquillo *(42)* Calmly.

Transcribing *(85–86)* Writing out the music of a performance you hear.

Transposing *(93–95)* Changing the key of a piece of music.

Transposing instruments *(13, 92–93)* A transposing

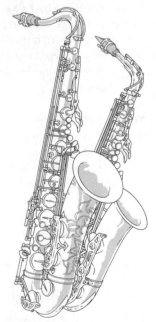

Saxophones are transposing instruments.

instrument sounds another note than the one the player reads and fingers. A B♭-instrument sounds a B♭ when you finger a C.

Treble clef *(10)* Another name for the G-clef. See: *Clef.*

Tremolo *(48, 49)* Quick repetition of one note, or rapid alternation between two notes.

Trill *(47)* Ornament: the word 'trill' about says it all.

Triple time *(19, 20)* Three beats per bar.

Triplet *(24–25)* A note divided into three equal parts.

Triplet feel See *Swing* and *Straight eighths.*

Tritone *(77)* Interval that spans three (tri) whole steps (tones), *e.g.*, C–F♯ or G–C♯.

Turn *(49–50)* Ornament: a turn around the note. Formally called a *grupetto.*

Unison *(73, 74)* 'One sound'. The smallest interval (*e.g.*, C–C).

Upbeat 1. *(96)* The opposite of a downbeat. See: Natural accents. 2. *(26)* Another word for pickup. See: *Pickup.*

Vibrato *(49)* Slight, rapid pitch fluctuation.

Vivace *(42)* Lively.

Weak beats *(96)* The first and third beat in a four-four bar. See: *Natural accents.*

White key, white note *(7)* The white keys of a keyboard instrument are also called white notes, or naturals.

Whole note *(16, 18)* Open-headed note without stem. Lasts four beats in $\frac{4}{4}$. Not to be confused with whole tone. See: *Whole step.*

Whole step *(7, 58–59)* A major second, equaling two half steps (from C to D, or from G♯ to A♯, for instance). Also known as *whole tone*, which should not be confused with a *whole note*: a note that lasts four counts or beats in $\frac{4}{4}$.

Whole tone See: *Whole step.*

Whole-tone scale *(90)* Scale made up entirely of whole step intervals. Also called *hexatonic scale.*

ESSENTIAL REFERENCE

In this chapter you'll find various things which are good to have at hand for immediate reference. This section includes the major and minor scales written out on staffs, a do-it-yourself scale wheel, the circle of fifths, some memory aids, and the system of naming specific notes and octaves.

Scale wheel

When photocopied and assembled, the scale wheel on the opposite page shows you the notes in each major and minor scale, and the names of the intervals within an octave.

Photocopy

Photocopy the two circles, cut them out, glue them onto card, and pin them together in the center. The outer part is a one-octave keyboard, made into a circle.

Scales

If you want to find out the notes of a major scale, point 'ROOT MAJOR' at the root note of the scale. The black arrows will point to the notes of the scale. For the minor scales use 'ROOT MINOR'.

Intervals

In order to read the name of an interval, point the 'ROOT MAJOR' at the lower notes, and read the abbreviated name of the interval which is pointing at the upper note. Maj. stands for major; min. stands for minor; aug. stands for augmented; dim. stands for diminished.

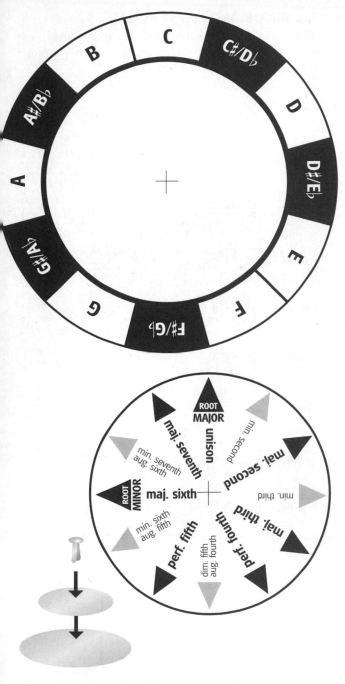

Photocopy this page, cut the circles out, and assemble them.

127

ALL MAJOR AND MINOR SCALES

The major and minor scales are the two most widely used scales in Western music. Here are the twenty-six most important ones, written out on a staff.

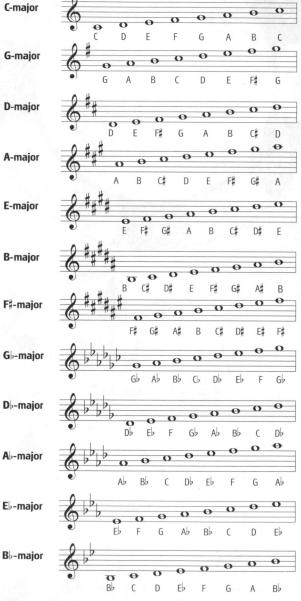

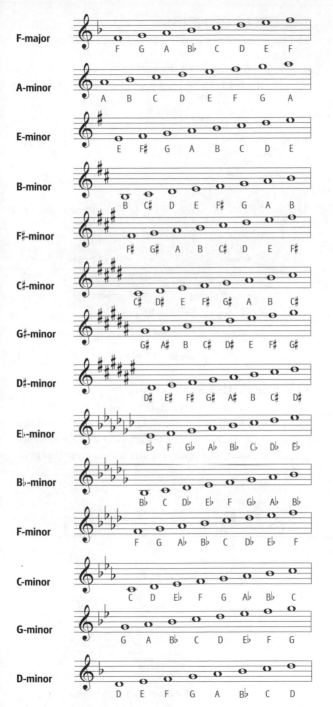

THE CIRCLE OF FIFTHS

You can read all about the circle of fifths in Chapters 11 and 13.

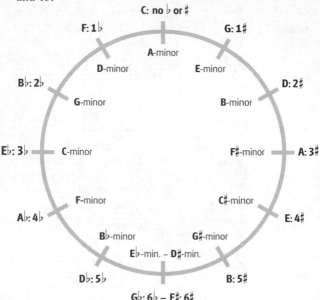

KEY SIGNATURES

The order of sharps and flats in the key signature is explained in Chapters 4, 10, and 11. Here's a memory aid to help you learn that order by heart. Note that the sentence for flats is exactly the reverse of the sentence for sharps.

Order of the sharps: *Father Charles Goes Down And Ends Battle*.

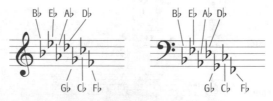

Order of the flats: *Battle Ends And Down Goes Charles Father*.

How many?

Two more memory aids, telling you the number of sharps and flats in each of the major scales:

Go (1) **D**own (2) **A**nd (3) **E**at (4) **B**aked (5) **F**ish (F♯: 6 sharps). The scale of G-major has one sharp, D-major has two, and so on.

Father (1) **B**ill (2) **E**ats (3) **A** (4) **D**ried (5) **G**rape (G♭: 6 flats). F-major has one flat, the B♭ has two, E♭ has three, and so on.

THE OCTAVES

A piano keyboard encompasses a little more than seven octaves. Consequently, you can play a C on eight different keys, from low to high. To distinguish the various octaves and keys, each has been numbered.

C1–C8

The first and lowest C on a piano, on the far left, is C1. The highest C, the very last key of the keyboard, is C8. Middle C, in the middle of the piano keyboard, is C4. On paper you'll find this note on a ledger line between the treble and bass staff.

Range

These octave and notes names are also used for other instruments and for singers – for example, to indicate their range or certain notes. The lowest string on a guitar is tuned to E2; the highest to E4. The A to which most orchestras and groups tune is A4.

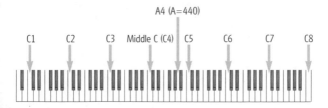

A4 (A=440)

C1 C2 C3 Middle C (C4) C5 C6 C7 C8

Other names

Occasionally, you may come across other systems of naming notes and octaves. Here are some examples.

Common notation	Helmholtz pitch notation	Alternative notation	Key numbers
C0–B0	C0–B0	CCCC	A0–B3
C1–B1	C1–B1	CCC	C4–B15
C2–B2	C–B	CC	C16–B27
C3–B3	c–b	C	C28–B39
C4–B4	c'–b' (or c1–b1)	c	C40–B51
C5–B5	c"–b" (or c2–b2)	c'	C52–B63
C6–B6	c'''–b''' (or c3–b3)	c"	C64–B75
C7–B7	c''''–b'''' (or c4–b4)	c'''	C76–B87
C8	c''''' (or c5)	c''''	C88

Hertz

The exact pitch of a note is determined by its frequency: the number of vibrations per second (Hertz or Hz). For A4 this number is usually 440, indicated as A=440 hertz, A=440Hz or simply A=440. Most orchestras and groups tune to this pitch. In some countries a slightly higher pitch is also used, *e.g.*, A=442 or A=444.